PENGUIN HANDBOOKS

THE PENGUIN GUIDE TO CHEAPER WINES

Paul Breman was born in 1931 and has been an antiquarian bookseller for most of his active life. He now specializes in books on architecture. What he calls his 'spare-time crazes' include publishing poetry by black authors, research into the history of English country houses, a book on the blues, four children of greatly varying ages, the bibliography of fortification, and a rock group. He writes that 'all of these activities improve with a glass of wine'.

For Penguins he has previously done a Dutch phrase book (in a series devised by his wife) and an anthology of black verse from three continents called *You Better Believe It*.

PAUL BREMAN

The Penguin Guide to

CHEAPER
WINES

PENGUIN BOOKS

Penguin Books Ltd, Harmondsworth, Middlesex, England
Penguin Books, 625 Madison Avenue, New York, New York 10022, U.S.A.
Penguin Books Australia Ltd, Ringwood, Victoria, Australia
Penguin Books Canada Ltd, 41 Steelcase Road West, Markham, Ontario, Canada
Penguin Books (N.Z.) Ltd, 182–190 Wairau Road, Auckland 10, New Zealand

—

First published 1976
Copyright © Paul Breman 1976

—

Made and printed in Great Britain by
Richard Clay (The Chaucer Press), Ltd
Bungay, Suffolk
Set in Monotype Ehrhardt

JMN AND ALL THE DAUGHTERS

This book is intended for those who already like drinking wine, but to whom the habit is new or the budget a factor which limits their choice. We all indulge the occasional spree on something we like, but everyday use is a much more serious matter. The wines discussed in this Guide could all be had at prices between 8op and £1.65 at the time I finished writing – by the time you have the book in your hands in-flation will no doubt have upped these figures somewhat. It will have upped everything else as well, including, I fear, our need for wine to cheer us.

The main aim of the book is to make sure you use what money you have to spend on wine as well as possible. What you consider your best buys will depend mostly on your own taste – this should always be the starting-point. When you drink something you like, find out what it is and where it comes from: it may have brothers and sisters, and some of these may please you as much or more. Start tasting wines, consciously, from whatever slender hold you've already established. Don't grab the nearest bottle off the nearest shelf just because the price suits you: next door there may be better for less.

Some of the wines you will find here you will have difficulty finding in your local shop, or within the price range mentioned. Here is your second hurdle: you not only have to use your own palate, you have to use your eyes as well – get to know the wine shops you have access to, compare their selection, find the one which is just that bit more adventurous and if you're at all lucky the manager will also be helpful. People in the wine trade are surprisingly helpful to anyone with a genuine interest. You will learn there are bin ends, and auctions, and clubs, and tastings, and all manner of means to assist your learning.

Eventually, I hope, you will also turn your thoughts to the future. What you will drink in five or ten years will depend a lot on what you do now. Not just on what you learn and how you develop your taste, but also on whether you can discipline yourself to put something by that is not for drinking now. Buying wine when it is too young to drink is the only thing most of us can afford to do – we should try to keep at least the more worthy ones as long as we can afford to, or we will never drink anything better than we deserve.

It was tempting, at first, to make this book more discursive, with longer and more general entries discussing the comparative merits of groups of wines (Spanish reds, or 'best buys to go with fish') or even the stimulating relationship between the landscape of a wine district and its products – but these temptations were resisted to provide a real guide which you can carry around to check the wines you find on an actual shop shelf. Almost all of the book, therefore, has the label on the bottle as its guiding principle: any word on a label that might convey some information about the bottle's content you should be able to find here, within certain limits – for instance, no words from languages which you will meet in their country of origin but seldom on the export market.

As for the practical information on specific wines: clearly it is impossible to list *every* wine that might be available on the British market. What you should be able to find is either the name of the grape variety which determines the style of the wine, or the place or region of origin. For the blended wines sold under proprietary names, which form an important sector of the cheaper market, I have tried to include comments on as many brand names as possible. The notes in most cases reflect my own taste, which may well be different from yours: check out a few wines you know well, and you will know how to interpret what I say about others.

'Wine', incidentally, has been taken to mean just what it says on page 152. This excludes anything not made from grapes. Apart from that, I have also kept down the entries on fortified wines.

Ultimately, a book like this has to explain *itself* even to the beginner, without any outside help. Cross-references have therefore been kept to a minimum: it should simply be assumed that *any* word used which is at all 'special' will be found defined under its own heading (this applies especially to the descriptive jargon which puzzles so many of us in merchants' and restaurant lists). The cross-references that remain all refer to specific information embedded in a more general entry.

A few abbreviations have been used, of which only two are important enough to merit a real explanation: AC and VDQS have been used, throughout, as the shortest indication of the 'status' of a wine, a dependability factor. These are terms one has to come to grips with sooner rather than later, and their explanation can be found under the headings they abbreviate: 'appellation contrôlée' and 'vin délimité de qualité supérieure'. The other abbreviations occur only in brackets at the beginning of short 'translations': F for French, G for German, H for Hungarian, I for Italian, P for Portuguese, R for Romanian and S for Spanish. Names of individual châteaux (not too many of these are included) will be found under the main name, not under Château.

A

abboccato. (I) Medium sweet, used of white wines like Orvieto.

Abfüllung. (G) Bottling.

abocado. (S) Medium sweet, used of sherry-type wines like Montilla.

Abzug. (G) Bottling.

AC. ⟡ appellation contrôlée.

acetic acid. This substance which eventually would turn wine into vinegar results from the oxidization of ethyl alcohol under the influence of a fungoid catalyst, *Mycoderma aceti*. Its presence is always harmful, unlike that of other acids such as tartaric acid.

Achaïa-Clauss. ⟡ Castel Danielis; Demestica.

acidity. Refers to the (very necessary) presence of fruit acids in wine. Without sufficient acidity the wine will not mature, but too much gives it an unripe, green or harsh taste.

acids. The main acids present in wine are acetic, malic and tartaric acid: see their separate entries.

adamado. (S and P) Medium sweet.

adega. (P) Cellar or store.

Adgestone. One of the best of the newer English vineyards, situated in the Isle of Wight. It produces a pleasant, very dry white wine from the excellent Seyve-Villard grapes which are gaining rapidly in popularity. Like all English wines, it is slightly too high in price for everyday use, but it does still have a certain amount of curiosity value.

age. Different wines are at their best at different ages, and much depends on their quality at the time of bottling. Very generally, light wines are drunk younger than the heavier ones. Equally generally, because of rising prices more and more wines are drunk younger than they should be – a dangerous practice which in future years will send the price of mature wines up even further.

German white wines are usually at their best in two to three years; most Italian whites (and those from farther east or south) do not improve with age at all. Burgundies need at least five to seven years, the great ones more than that. Good clarets will keep longest, and those of the Haut-Médoc especially may not be anywhere near their best under fifteen or twenty years.

Ahr. Along this small tributary which runs into the Rhine opposite Ling lies the smallest German wine district. It is the only one known mostly for its red wines.

Aigues-Mortes. ⟡ vin des sables.

Ain-Bessem. ⟡ Algeria.

alb. (R) White.

alcohol. Properly called ethyl alcohol, a colourless liquid with a faint smell most people seem to like. It is the 'active' ingredient in all alcoholic drinks. In wine, it is formed by yeast cells which change the fructose of the must to alcohol and carbon dioxide. The alcoholic strength of wines varies: table wines will usually be 10 or 11 per cent, but those from hot dry regions often reach 13 per cent or more. Fortified wines have their alcohol content raised artificially.

Aleatico. A black muscat grape grown in Apulia, Umbria, Lazio (the Castelli Romani vineyards) and on Elba. Its sweet red wines are usually named after the grape, with additions like 'di Puglia' denoting the place of origin.

Alella. A very plain, refreshing white ordinary, named after a village just north-east of Barcelona and sold in characteristic long, fluted bottles. The name is much abused for less pleasant wines, for instance on Menorca.

Algeria. The vine returned to islamic Algeria as early as the 1840s, and within a few decades the country produced about a million hectolitres. Most of it was sold to France for blending into red 'ordinaires', but a dozen mountain wines reached VDQS status. Some of these have survived the loss of the French market, which is only partly compensated for by other exports, and continue to maintain or improve their standards. Oran province still produces about two-thirds of the country's total, but the better wines come from the coastal region east of the city, the Dahra hills and their continuation the Zaccar hills. South-east of Algiers is Ain-Bessem, where the limestone soil makes particularly good fruity and dark rosés. In Oran province itself Mascara and the Tessala mountains make the best wines.

Aliança. Brand name for some very good wines from the rather neglected Barraida region of coastal Portugal.

Aligoté. Name of a white grape widely used in Burgundy. Inferior in quality to the Chardonnay, its wines do not improve much in the bottle.

Allander. Brand name of the House of Fraser (better known for running Harrods) for three ordinaries, rather confusingly marketed either in standard bottles labelled 'produce of France' or in double-litres saying 'vino da pasto' from the hills of Verona.

all'annata. (I) 'Of the year': wine drunk young, in the year after the vintage.

Almadén. The Almadén vineyards in California were established in the 1840s by a farmer from Bordeaux: thirty years later they were the largest in the state. They have since moved farther south into the Salinas valley, beyond

Soledad, because their original location at Los Gatos in the Santa Cruz hills has been swamped by the sprawling suburbs of San José. The product ranges from sparkling Blanc de Blancs ('bottle fermented', as the Americans say, from Chardonnay grapes) to sherries made by the proper flor and solera system. The Mountain Reds are especially good, and several of the varietal wines are America's staple drinking diet. Presumably it will not be long before we see them cross the ocean.

Aloxe-Corton. Aloxe is a beautiful little village in the hills just before Beaune, off the dreary road from Dijon. Its vineyards slope down to that road from the Bois de Corton: the higher ones are the best, and it is from one of these that the hyphenated addition to the village name is taken. The few whites are as beautiful as the place, but prohibitively expensive. The reds are very high on my own list of favourites, but only when they have reached a venerable age.

Alsace. The easternmost province of France, between the Rhine valley and the Vosges mountains, has only recently started making quality wines. Earlier, from before its German period until well into the 1920s, it made stupendous quantities (a quarter of the entire German output) but nothing of individual note. Now it makes smaller amounts of dry but fragrant white wines of very consistent quality (chaptalization is allowed here). The wines are known by varietal names, not much by place or vineyard. Grown on limestone and granite soils they are based on six official 'cépages nobles': Riesling, Gewürztraminer, Muscat, Pinot Blanc and Gris, and Sylvaner. These varietal names also account for six of the nine ACs granted only as late as 1962. The other three are Alsace, Edelzwicker and, for pink wines, Pinot Noir. Quality is guaranteed more by the producer's or shipper's name than by anything else. In Britain, the names Hugel and (in various permutations) Dopff dominate the market.

Alto Adige. The upper reaches of the Adige valley, also known as the Italian Tirol. It is the home of the Traminer grape (named after a village some ten miles south of Bolzano), but its best wines are made from another local white grape, the Schiava. The best known of these, Lago di Caldara or Kalterersee, was the region's only DOC, but more will be granted in the near future. As in southern Switzerland, the Merlot makes very soft red wines, and of the various Pinots used, the only one repaying the trouble is the Pinot Grigio or Ruländer.

amabile. (I) Gentle, that is to say, medium sweet. Often used for red wines as abboccato is for whites.

amaro. (I) 'Bitter', but also used to denote very dry wine.

Ambra. One of the more reliable names in the Italian double-litre export trade. Most of the wines sold under this label come from northern Italy (red Bardolino and Valpolicella, white Soave and an 'Italian rosé' of unspecified antecedents) but the best one is the dry white Frascati.

Amontillado. A sherry made by ageing Finos in wood. It remains dry, but is darker in colour and has a stronger, mellower flavour.

Amoroso. Full and sweetish sherry which André Simon described as 'best served with turtle soup'.

amtliche Prüfungs-Nummer. An official test number which all German wines of Qualitätswein class and over are required to show on the label. Its three groups of figures are codes for harvest control, analysis and taste control. Unintelligible and of no interest to the buyer of everyday wine.

Anbaugebiet. (G) ⇨ Gebiet.

Anjou. As a wine-producing area Anjou coincides roughly with the official department Maine-et-Loire, across the river from Angers (which has no vineyards at all). The

Pineau grape makes fine, naturally sweet wines in tributary river valleys like the Coteaux du Layon, and the Cabernet makes the area's most famous wines: Rosé d'Anjou, Cabernet rosé d'Anjou, Anjou-Coteaux de la Loire and Cabernet de Saumur. The production of these popular pink wines increases rapidly, and seems likely to crowd out a few of the region's better but less lucrative wines.

Apetlon. Village in Austria, south-east of Vienna, near the Hungarian border. The Rheinriesling grape here produces very good white wines, especially sweet ones.

Aphrodite. A pleasant light white table wine from Cyprus, named after the goddess of love, who is said to have been born (if that is the word) on the island's south coast.

A.P.Nr. ⟡ amtliche Prüfungs-Nummer.

appellation contrôlée. (F) Legal guarantee of the origin and production standards of French wines, administered by I.N.A.O., the Institut National des Appellations d'Origine, in Paris. Very strictly upheld, especially as regards the quantity which any particular area is allowed to market under the AC. Before the U.K.'s entry into the Common Market, French wine laws did not apply here, and shippers could buy the 'surplus' quantities for sale at lower prices but under their original names: this is no longer permitted. Wine produced in excess of the AC amounts begins to be marketed as Rouge de ... and Blanc de ... with the name of the grower: this way, even the actual vineyard can be named without legal problems.

Meanwhile, the AC scene changes year by year, as wines are reclassified or moved up from the second rank (⟡ vin délimité de qualité supérieure). At present nearly 15 per cent of France's total wine production has the right to an AC.

Apremont. Dry, crisp, very light white wine from Savoy, near the famous vermouth town of Chambéry. It is made from a local grape called Jacquère.

Apulia. ⟡ Aleatico; Malvasia.

Aragon. ⟡ Cariñeña; Vista.

Aral. Name of the biggest wine-producing firm of Turkey. Like most Turkish producers, it does not own vineyards but simply processes grapes from anywhere.

Arbois. ⟡ Jura; vin fou.

Argentina. With a steadily increasing industry, Argentina is already the fourth largest wine producer in the world. Even so, home consumption leaves little for export. Almost three-quarters of the present 310,000 hectares of vineyard are in Mendoza province, at the extreme west of the country, on the same latitude as the centre of Chilean wine production on the other side of the Andes mountains. The rest of the vineyards are mostly in San Juan, just north of Mendoza. The Criolla grape covers one-fifth of the total acreage and produces pink wines which bear its name. Next in popularity is the Malbec, giving a wine of full colour and body, and high alcohol content. Pedro Ximenez is the most used grape for white wines. Despite an annual rainfall about one-quarter of that of Bordeaux the yield per acre is high – but irrigation does not improve quality.

Shipments of wine are in bulk even within the country: most of the bottling is done in Buenos Aires. The Peñaflor concern is the world's third largest producer; its main blending tank holds 52,000 hectolitres. The only Argentinian blend widely available in the U.K. is variously called Franchette or Ruiz Belmonte. Most of the better wines available here are Cabernets from Mendoza and a few mixed-grape reds like the Greco Brothers' 'Cuevas viejas', Furlotti's strong 'Tinto reserva' and José Orfila's 'Borgogna'.

Armenia. That part of the country which is now one of the Soviet Republics is among the older wine-producing regions in the world. At present it caters to the general Russian demand for sweet and dessert wines, but some drier ones find their way out of the country and are worth tracking down.

aroma. 'Roughly speaking the smell of the taste, whilst bouquet is the impersonal collection of smells ... recognized by the nose alone' (Sichel, *Penguin Book of Wines*, page 39).

asciutto. (I) Dry. Used mostly for Sicilian wines, but also for Frascati.

Assmannshausen. On the Rhine below Bingen, the farthest outposts of the Rheingau vineyards, and the only one among them that is famous for its red wines rather than the usual whites. Its grape is the Spätburgunder, and I find the dry red produced from it much more likeable than the overrated sweetish pink version.

Asti Spumante. The best-known sparkling wine of Italy. Made in the Piedmont from Muscat grapes by a process which differs from those used in France: here the carbon dioxide is developed during the first fermentation in a closed vat. This preserves the characteristic taste of the Muscat's natural sugar. The result is rather sweet but fresh and delicate as well. There is much difference between the various manufacturers' product; the only one I really like is Gancia. Recently the price of Asti has gone up as a result of increased duty which now stands at nearly 60p a bottle.

Astra. Brand name for a large range of mostly white Romanian wines, including not only the usual export varietals like Cabernet, Traminer and Riesling, but also more exclusive wines. The Perla is a pleasant, only slightly sweet speciality of the Tîrnăve region of Transylvania. The dry Rulanda (after the German name of the Pinot Gris) presumably comes from the south-east, as does the luscious dessert wine of Murfatlar. The Muscat, surprisingly good if you like Muscat at all, is made from the Balkan variety of the grape, the Muscat Ottonel.

astringent. The mouth-puckering sensation given by wines of high tannin content.

aszu. (H) 'Selected' (that is late-gathered, overripe) grapes, often affected by noble rot. These are kneaded rather than pressed into a strong, sweet paste which is added to one-year-old Tokay in varying percentages expressed on the label in 'puttonyok' (the number of standard vats of aszu added to the much larger fermenting tank of the Tokay).

Auberge. Brand name used by Charles Kinloch for low-priced French wines of AC standards. The range is unusual for including a Bordeaux Clairet: the pink Bordeaux entitled to this appellation is seldom seen in the U.K., even if we derived our word claret from its name. The Auberge clairet is quite a nice one.

auctions. The two big London auction houses, Sotheby's and Christie's, both conduct regular sales of wines, as do some smaller firms, not all of them in London. At Christie's a large percentage is reasonably cheap. It comes from bin ends, defunct merchants' stocks, small importers who find auctions a convenient outlet, or even 'dumping' by shippers with overstock in times of market crisis (the 1975–6 auction season has seen a massive unloading of 1970 claret at very reasonable prices). The quantity in any one lot is seldom less than three cases of a dozen bottles each (except for the grander wines) and often it is as high as ten cases. Most of it is bought by the trade, and therefore a private buyer can find some really competitive prices here. To combat the quantity factor it is good to assemble a small group of like-minded drinkers to share purchases.

Much wine is offered 'unlabelled', 'without capsules', or in bond. This tends to discourage the small private buyer but it should not, for here are the bargains for those with courage. Tastings are held before each sale, and the thing is to trust your own palate and stick with it rather than pay attention solely to names on labels. Mind the lots marked in the catalogue with a dagger: they are trade stock and VAT has to be added to their auction price.

Aude. One of the largest wine-producing regions in France, producing enormous quantities of undistinguished reds and a few better ones like Corbières and Minervois which are coming into their own as honest cheap wines.

aus eigenem Lesegut. (G) From the producer's own vineyards.

Auslese. (G) Wine made from late-gathered grapes, with all unripe grapes removed. This is the highest rank of Qualitätswein one can find within the price range of this guide.

Australia. Cultivation of the vine goes back surprisingly far in Australia, to the First Fleet in fact, but the production of acceptable table wines in any quantity is comparatively recent. Half the grape crop is distilled for industrial alcohol, and for a long time the only wines made were sweet or fortified. This has changed dramatically in the last ten years, under the combined onslaught of public demand and increased production control. The wine-producing areas are roughly on the same latitude as the Mediterranean and North Africa, and their wines naturally tend to be high on sugar, low on acids: the balance has to be restored artificially, by the addition of tartaric acid and sometimes tannin. On the whole, the red wines are the best, but the cooler valleys (especially Hunter and Barossa) make good whites as well. The main grapes are the European varieties best suited to the climate: white and black Hermitage (that is, Ugni Blanc and Syrah or Shiraz), Cabernet and Sémillon. Most of the vineyards are on the Adelaide side of South Australia (but Coonawarra in the extreme south makes the best reds of the whole country) and in New South Wales

north of Sydney. Several of the wine areas are remote
enough to have escaped phylloxera, but those of the biggest
producer of the time, Victoria, never quite recovered.
Recently new tax regulations have dealt a heavy blow which
will undoubtedly be reflected in the prices which are already too high for the U.K. market.

Austria. Produces a variety of white wines mostly in the
Wachau, around Vienna, and in Burgenland. Very few of
them travel well (in fact, a great many do not take too well
to being bottled at all), but the late-gathered Beerenausleses
are an exception. These excellent sweet wines are, however,
outside our price range. Austrian wine laws being very lax
indeed, there is no guarantee that the grapes used for
'Austrian wine' were actually grown in the country.

Auxey-Duresses. Small village in the Côte de Beaune, with
its own AC. Not much known and therefore sometimes
quite cheap. Good reds, but the whites are nowhere near
the quality of neighbouring Meursault.

Aveleda. A white Vinho Verde of better than average quality,
which comes in an unusual tall bottle with a Pre-Raphaelite
label.

Avensan. A small commune in the Haut-Médoc next to
Moulis: good if rather harsh cru bourgeois wines dominated
by those of Château Citran.

Azerbaijan. This continuation of Georgia's southern slopes
of the Caucasus is another of the very old wine-producing
regions where viticulture went rather literally underground,
the vineyards being dug up after the advent of abstaining
Islam, to be revived in the nineteenth century. Most of its
present production is what the Russians call 'Portvein'
(which tastes about the same as it sounds) but a few good
wines reach the export market. Matrasa is a smooth red and
Bayan Shirei a light white table wine which need no
apology.

B

Badacsony. The volcanic hillsides of Mount Badacsony near Lake Balaton in Hungary produce two rather fierce white wines from native grapes which give them their names: Badacsonyi Szürkebarat and the even better Badacsonyi Kéknyelü. Both go well with spicy food.

Bad Dürkheim. Centre of wine production in the Mittel-haardt, and the biggest commune in all of Germany. Its own wines (both red and white) are reliable but of no great distinction: the best stretch of the area ends a few miles south, at Wachenheim.

Baden. The southernmost and sunniest German wine district, north of Switzerland and east of Alsace. It is divided into eight regions which produce very different wines from very different grapes. The best of them come from a small volcanic region called the Kaiserstuhl, while the Mark-gräferland (between Freiburg and Basel) makes drinkable whites from the Chasselas grape. Good white wines also come from the Ortenau region, where Durbach, Neuweier and Schloss Staufenberg are the best-known names. Among the many red wines of Baden those made from the Spät-burgunder are easily the best.

balance. The relation between sugar and acidity in a wine. The actual proportions will vary drastically in different wines, but they all have a point where they are 'just right'.

Balaton. The northern shores of the huge Lake Balaton, south-west of Budapest, are covered with vineyards which thrive both in the climate (hot summers tempered by a large expanse of water) and in the soil – a sandy basalt with volcanic outcrops. Balatoni Riesling is the best-known product abroad, a fresh dry white which is at its best when very young. Balatoni Furmint is rather more special and powerful.

Balls Brothers. ♦ Choix du Roy; Cuvée Sérain; Jour de Fête; Plonque.

Bandol. One of only four A C districts in Provence, growing a variety of grapes dominated by the local Mourvèdre, mostly on very steep slopes of limestone or even flint. The reds are soft, subtle and on the whole long-lasting; the pinks much firmer and tastier than those of the Rhône. Their price is already high for wine from this part of France.

Banyuls. ♦ Roussillon.

Barbaresco. A Piedmont red, made from Nebbiolo grapes. Full-bodied, deep in colour, and fragrant: a cheaper and commoner version of the great Barolo.

Barbe, Château de. ♦ Côtes de Bourg.

Barbera. Name of a black grape grown extensively in northern Italy (it is the most used grape in Piedmont) and also in California. By extension, the name of wines made from this grape. The best (Barbera d'Asti) is quite a pleasant table wine, a bit like Rhône wines – but beware the sweet version (Barbera amabile) which I find nauseating.

Bardolino. One of the better red Italian table wines, light and bright, dry and fresh. It is made from a variety of grapes grown on the eastern shore of Lake Garda. Usually drunk young and slightly chilled.

Barolo. After Chianti, this is the best known of Italy's few great red wines. It is made in Piedmont, near Alba, from Nebbiolo grapes. Full-bodied, fragrant, and a deep dark red, it ages as well and often as long as good Bordeaux. It is seldom found at an accessible price any more (not even in Italy) but it is worth looking out for in bin ends and auctions. Give it at least ten years to develop.

Barossa Valley. The larger of Australia's best wine regions, this valley of the Para river lies about forty miles north-east of Adelaide. Its vineyards were started by German immigrants and still specialize in 'Riesling' wines. Gramp's Orlando in Barossa Valley itself and Hamilton's Springton vineyards in neighbouring Eden Valley dominate the region, for quality rather than quantity.

Barraida. ◊ Aliança; Portugal.

Barrera. Brand name used by Finch for Spanish wines sold cheaply in litre bottles. The red is none too likeable and I find the sweet white equally dubious. The dry white which completes the range is much better if still no more than an honest ordinaire. It alone goes under the name Vinado – presumably someone's unhappy way of anglicizing viñedo.

Barsac. One of the five communes which make up the Sauternes district. The other four all use the AC Sauternes, but this northern end of the region, above the little Ciron river, is entitled to use its own name. It makes the same luscious white wines, but perhaps just slightly drier and with a distinctive bouquet. In the cheaper versions which concern us most, this distinction is not nearly so pronounced and the wine is often indifferent, though seldom as unpleasant as cheap Sauternes from farther south.

Baton. Brand name of Evans Marshall (London) for French wines which are slightly nearer to rock-bottom in quality than in price.

Baumé scale. Like Oechsle, this is a measure for the sugar content of wine. One degree B is equivalent roughly to 18 grammes of sugar per litre: such a wine would be medium dry. Two degrees B is medium sweet, 3° sweet. Dessert wines go up to 5°.

Bayan Shirei. ⋄ Azerbaijan.

Beaujolais. An area of granite hills forty-five miles long and barely eight miles wide, south of the Mâconnais and therefore the southernmost part of what is so loosely known as Burgundy. This region produces nearly as much wine as all the Bordeaux fine wine regions put together, but most of it is very ordinary. The Gamay is its great grape; its wines are deep in colour but light in body, rather high in alcohol content (Beaujolais Supérieur derives its superiority from an extra 1 per cent) and famous the world over as 'easy drinkers' because they happen to be both inviting and actually thirst-quenching. It has long been the one well-known French wine without real standards: nobody cared much what exactly went into it. A small area in the north-west of the region makes wine of higher than average quality and stricter controls (⋄ next entry).

Nearly all Beaujolais matures quickly and only a few are thought to improve with age beyond the first three years. A speciality of the region is 'Beaujolais nouveau', the very fresh new wine which can be sold from 15 November after the vintage and is the object of highly organized races to Paris, London and elsewhere. The sale, at lower prices, of 'Beaujolais de l'année' in the New Year is pretentious in view of the fact that most Beaujolais is drunk before the next vintage anyway.

Beaujolais-Villages. In the north-west of the Beaujolais district thirty-five villages are entitled to this AC which is meant to express some superiority over the ordinary wines of the region. Nine of these communes in fact never use any name but their own: these are the grands crus of Beaujolais. From heaviest to lightest they are: Moulin à Vent, Juliénas, Morgon, Fleurie, Chénas, Côte de Brouilly, Brouilly, Saint-Amour and Chiroubles. All will be found under their own separate entries.

Beaulieu vineyard

Beaulieu vineyard. ◊ Napa Valley.

Beaumes-de-Venise. North of Carpentras and east of Orange, this commune makes a dessert wine which is reckoned to be the best sweet Muscat of France.

Beaune. The active centre of the Côte de Beaune vineyards, a town one can call picturesque if looking no farther than the roof of the Hospice but which is really just a hustling market town with pretensions that keep pace with its rapidly rising prices. Its own wines are all rated as premier cru – it is perhaps unfair to remember that it was the town itself that had most of the early classifications in its giving. The simple place-name is the lowest A C of the region, used for soft red and some fine white wines.

Beau-Site, Château. ◊ Saint-Estèphe.

Beerenauslese. ◊ Qualitätswein mit Prädikat.

Bellapais. An unusual slightly sparkling wine from an unusual part of Cyprus: the north coast, near Kyrenia.

Ben Ean. ◊ Hunter Valley.

Bereich. (G) Specific district within a larger wine-producing region or Gebiet.

Bergerac. The large wine-growing region around Bergerac on the Dordogne, in the heart of the Périgord, is known mostly for its white wines. These are either dry and indifferent, or sweet and indifferent. Its red wines, lighter and rather softer than the neighbouring clarets, are beginning to come into their own as dependable drinking wines at reasonable prices. Pécharmant, made in the direct environment of Bergerac itself, is said to be the best of them.

Bernkastel. On the right bank of the Moselle, joined with its suburb Kues across the river by a bridge which (towards Graach) affords probably the most spectacular view of vineyard country anywhere in the world. Bernkasteler wines are almost colourless, which makes the contrast with their strong scent and luscious yet sharp taste all the stronger. Most are marketed under two rather all-embracing names: Schwanen and Badstube, the latter being the better. The most famous single vineyard, the Doktor (from Doktor Thanisch, whose firm is still an active producer-shipper), faces due south on a steep hill just above the village.

bianco. (I) White.

Bikavér. ◊ Bull's Blood; Szekszárd.

bin. The place in which bottled wine is kept in a cellar. If a particular bin number is quoted, it should guarantee the uniform quality of wine bottled and laid down on the same day.

bin ends. When the quantity left in stock of a particular wine is too low to warrant inclusion in the next list or catalogue (because the wine would be sold out long before the list was due for revision) both caterers and merchants tend to sell these 'ends' at reduced prices. Hotels and restaurants often do this by special offer to parties of the right size or by putting lots of better wines up for auction, but it is worth looking out for the bin end offers of your local merchant.

Blagny. This tiny village suffers from the reputation of its neighbours, Puligny-Montrachet and Meursault. Its white wines, in fact, usually go under the name of Meursault. The reds, however, have Blagny as their own AC. They are rather soft, with a fine bouquet, and deserve to be better known.

blanc. (F) White.

Blanc de Blancs. Wine made from white grapes only. This is of special significance for Champagne, because the ones made solely from the Chardonnay grape are lighter and more delicate. The term itself is general and may be used of still as well as sparkling wines.

blanco. (S) White.

Blanquette. ◊ Limoux.

Blauburgunder. A German variety of Pinot Noir.

blend. A mixture of different wines or different vintages of the same wine, usually made to maintain a fairly uniform quality. Practically all Champagnes are blended, and so are several other wines, notably those of Alsace (◊ Zwicker). The most famous blended still wine is, of course, port.

Boal. ◊ Bual.

Bocksbeutel. (G) A flat bottle of dark green glass (flatter and wider than the kind known in the U.K. from Mateus Rosé) used for bottling the better wines of Franken.

bodega. (S) Store where wine is either kept or made; also, a wine bar.

Bodenheim. Northernmost wine-producing village of Rheinhessen.

body. The combination of alcohol content, grape sweetness and flavour which makes one wine appear more substantial or formidable than another.

bond. The cellar or warehouse in which imported wine is kept until the Customs & Excise duty has been paid. Also called a 'bonded warehouse'.

Bon Esprit. Brand name of Charles Kinloch (London) for three colours of French ordinaire which are all right for their price. The white tastes as if it comes from the deep south rather than the usual Loire.

Bonnezaux. ◊ Coteaux du Layon.

Bordeaux. Hugh Johnson, in the one piece of wine literature which is indispensable for all serious beginners (*The World Atlas of Wine*, published by Mitchell Beazley, London, 1971), says: 'Bordeaux is the largest fine-wine district on earth. The whole département of the Gironde, where the waters of the Dordogne and the

Garonne unite to flow into the Bay of Biscay, is dedicated to wine-growing. All its wine is Bordeaux.' Bordeaux and Bordeaux Supérieur, therefore, are the most general appellations to which nearly all the wine of the region is entitled. Further distinctions are of two kinds. First of all there is the clear distinction between the red wine districts in the north, on the right bank of the Dordogne and the left bank of the Gironde, and the white wine districts in the south, on the left banks of Garonne and Dordogne. Second to this still very general division is the strict hierarchy established in the various districts between their individual communes and estates. Details of this second classification will be found under the entry cru classé; more detailed information on the red wine regions under Médoc, Haut-Médoc, Graves, Premières Côtes de Bordeaux, Côtes de Bourg, Canon-Fronsac, Pomerol and Saint-Émilion; and notes on the white wine regions under Graves, Sauternes, Entre-deux-mers and Côtes de Blaye.

Borgogna. A full-bodied red wine from San Martin in the south-east of Mendoza province, Argentina. In spite of its name, it is made mostly from the claret grapes Merlot and Malbec and it is kept in oak for at least three years before bottling, like the similar wines of Spain's Rioja region.

bottle. Present-day wine bottles are nearly all of glass, cylindrical, with a narrow neck stopped with a cork. The standard size holds about seven-tenths of a litre; other much-used sizes are litres, magnums or 'doubles' (holding two bottles, or a litre and a half) and double-litres.

The more important variants on the standard shape are the following:

Burgundy bottle – broad with sloping shoulders. Similar bottles are used for Loire wines.

Bordeaux bottle – long neck, clearly defined shoulders which help keep back sediment while pouring. Green glass for red wines, clear for whites is standard practice with both these types.

Hock bottle – tall and slender, tapering upward rather than having any shoulders at all. Green glass for Alsace and Moselle, brown for Rhine wines.

Flask – round-bottomed and usually straw-covered (the bottle itself would not stand up), used mostly in Tuscany.

Bocksbeutel – almost circular from the front but flat from the sides, with a small oval base. Used in Germany for Frankenwein. Slightly thicker variants are used in Portugal for Vinho Verde and some pink wines, and in Italy.

bottle fermented. ◊ Almadén; méthode champenoise.

Boulaouane. ◊ Morocco.

bouquet. The smell of wine, largely due to the oxidization of some of the acids. It follows that wines of low acidity (Italian ones, for instance) have less of a bouquet than those with a high acidity like most German wines.

Bourgeuil. Pleasant red table wine from the Loire, twenty-five miles west of Tours. A little heavier than Chinon, it often ages very well. It is usually drunk at cellar temperature rather than chambré.

Bourgogne Aligoté. The white wines made anywhere in Burgundy from the Aligoté grape instead of the noble Chardonnay are never entitled to more than this, their own AC. Rightly so, my own taste confirms, for they are often thin and harsh.

Bouzy. The only place in the Champagne district to make a very good red wine from the Pinot Noir grapes grown here in such abundance. It is also used as the colourant in pink Champagne.

branco. (P) White.

brand names. Since Britain's entry into the Common Market the continental wine laws have started to apply here, too, and a golden era of rules-dodging has come to an end. We used to be able to buy wines which in France, say, were surplus to the quantities allowed under A C rules and which therefore in their country of origin could not be sold under their money-fetching name: here they could, and at lower prices. No more. The same wines continue to come, continue to be cheap – but their names have changed from generic ones to varietal (grape) names or often to brand names. Your wine merchant will still tell you what was what, otherwise you must go by your own taste and not by the label.

Another kind of brand name has come up: those used by chain stores, supermarkets and some wholesalers to cover a whole range of wines, blended from the produce of various regions, sometimes even different countries. To clear at least a bit of this new jungle I have included notes about more than eighty of these. Here more than anywhere the help and further comments of readers are urgently needed.

Brolio. ⇨ Chianti.

Brouilly. Biggest and southernmost of the nine crus of Beaujolais. Its wine is rather fuller than average but quick to mature. The best wine, from a small 'classico' area, has the appellation Côte de Brouilly.

brut. (F) Really and truly dry: said of a natural Champagne which has not been sweetened.

Bual. Name of the grape from which a sweet Madeira dessert wine is made.

Bulgaria. Has created an enormous wine industry out of virtually nothing in a remarkably short time, and now vies with Romania for sixth or seventh place in the world production table. Highly mechanized, it sets itself equally high standards and allows only a fraction of its wines to be classified even as table wines (leaving an endless quantity of unclassed sweet wine for consumption in the Soviet Union). The grapes used are mostly traditional and more-

or-less native: Gamza for dry reds which are lighter than their colour suggests, Dimiat for pleasant dry whites. Both often carry the district of origin after the grape name. Of the French grapes used, the Chardonnay usually gives the best wine, the Cabernet surprisingly sweet ones. Most of these are available already, and eventually we may see the dark fruity Mavrud wines here as well.

bulk process. ◊ cuve close.

Bull's Blood. A robust red wine from Kadarka grapes, made at Eger, one of Hungary's most important wine centres (halfway between Budapest and Tokay). Egri Bikavér, as it is called at home, ages well and really comes into its own at eight to twelve years. In the U.K. it is one of the very cheapest of honest and full-bodied red wines available.

Burgenland. The wines of this area of Austria around the Neusiedler See are very similar in character to those of the Hungarian Sopron district just across the border. Rust and Apetlon, on opposite sides of the lake, produce its best wines (all whites) from Rheinriesling and Furmint grapes. The reds, from Blauburgunder and Portugieser grapes, are full-bodied and rather heavy.

Burgundy. No longer in any sense a coherent province, and even in wine terms a conglomerate rather than an entity, 'Burgundy' is made up of six regions which fall into three wholly unrelated groups. Chablis is the most northerly, a white wine region north of Auxerre. About a hundred kilometres to the south-east is Dijon and the start of the next group, Côte de Nuits and Côte de Beaune, the 'classico' region known collectively as the Côte d'Or. The southern extension of this region is the Côte Chalonnaise. Much farther south, on the right bank of the Saône from Tournus almost to Lyon, are the Mâconnais and the Beaujolais regions, using different grapes on a different soil. The only common denominator between these very unalike regions is the exquisitely fragmented ownership of their vineyards. The most famous example is Clos de Vougeot, 124 acres of high-class vineyard with a well-known and high-priced product, worked in two-acre lots by more than sixty owners.

Buzbağ. A dark red wine from Anatolia in the heart of Turkey.

C

Cabaret. Brand name for 'medium dry' and 'full medium sweet' white wines and for a 'soft round medium dry' red, all from the Bergerac area. Nothing wrong with them, but not stuff you can drink for very long.

Cabernet. One of the most widely used grape families. Thin-skinned, blue-black, hardy and thriving on almost any soil the Cabernets with their high tannin content make excellent table wines which improve with age.

Cabernet Franc. This lesser relative of the Cabernet Sauvignon grape is much used in the Bordeaux regions, with the exception of the Médoc. It is also responsible for most of the Cabernet rosés of the Loire and elsewhere.

Cabernet Sauvignon. The aristocrat of the Cabernet family, taking credit for the best red wines of Bordeaux and especially the Médoc. It thrives in the climate of coastal California, where its ability to withstand the effects of damp on its ripe grapes stands it in good stead. In Chile its wines are remarkably like those of Bordeaux, in Australia they tend to be much darker, in South Africa and the Balkan countries they are singularly undistinguished.

Cabinet. (G) Formerly, a 'special reserve' denoting a higher than average quality. No longer used, in fact illegal. The present name Kabinett has a different meaning, ⋄ Qualitätswein mit Prädikat.

Cadillac. ⋄ Loupiac.

Cahors. Name of the one truly 'black' wine of all dark

French reds, produced in the Lot region around Cahors, mainly from the Malbec grape. A pleasant wine, only recently promoted to AC status, at its best after perhaps five years but with an amazing ability to keep. It is common in the regional restaurants to be offered a choice of vintages from the 1880s on – the older ones are not much more expensive but no better either; in the U.K. their price tends to be exaggerated.

California. California has an expanding wine industry with long traditions (only temporarily marred by prohibition, and not at all by phylloxera) and very high standards. An increasing quantity of dependable, cheap to medium wines for everyday drinking makes up the bulk of its production, but the more individual top range can stand comparison with the better wines of any country.

There is a marked difference between the coastal vineyards with their sea-tempered climate and those situated between the Coastal Range and the Sierra Nevada mountains where without special techniques it would be too dry and hot for anything but very ordinary wines. The best wine country is near San Francisco: the Napa Valley (north) and those of Livermore (east) and Salinas (south). The latter is dominated by the giant Almadén (now operated by National Distillers) and old reliable firms like Paul Masson.

California uses mostly European grape varieties, especially Grenache and Cabernet Sauvignon among the reds, the indifferent Colombard and Chenin Blanc together with very good Chardonnay among the whites. By far the greatest single acreage, however, is given to California's own mystery grape, the Zinfandel. Its dry red wines are used mostly for blending.

Cambas. ⟡ Greece.

Camel. ⟡ Israel.

Campania. This region around Naples consists of rich volcanic hills (Vesuvius) which run out to sea only to come up again as the islands of Capri and Ischia. Although most of the vineyards produce both white and red wine, it is usually the white which is better – and of these, Lacrima Christi is the most widely known and exported.

Cannonau. ◊ Sardinia.

Cannstatt. ◊ Württemberg.

Canon-Fronsac. The banks of the Dordogne just down-stream from Fronsac produce pleasantly fruity red wines much like those of the Saint-Émilion region, but perhaps a little lighter and fully mature in as little as ten years. The many smallish vineyards here and in the higher region known as Côtes de Fronsac are still among the cheapest of clarets but will not be so for much longer.

Canteloup, Château. ◊ Saint-Estèphe.

Cantenac. ◊ Margaux.

Canteval. Brand name of Nicolas for a light and well-balanced blend of French and Algerian reds. Such blends used to be common in France, but few have survived the upheavals of Algerian independence.

cantina. (I) Cellar or winery.

cantina cooperativa, cantina sociale. (I) A wine-producers' co-operative.

Capital Wine & Travers. ◊ Fleuron; Salvo; Taluna.

Capri. A pale, dry and quite fresh white wine. The name can quite officially be applied to wine from Capri itself, Ischia and part of the Campania mainland: soil, climate and grapes are identical. There is a red which is brightly coloured, soft and pleasant, and a rosé which fortunately one sees but seldom.

carafe. Not a fixed measure, but a word which has come into widespread use to describe what was known as an 'open' wine, i.e. one sold from the cask or other bulk container rather than in bottles. In most halfway decent restaurants, the 'carafe wines' are good value. If you come across one you particularly like, don't fail to ask what it really is. The open wines sold in U.K. pubs are a different story: they usually come from bottles of the nastier proprietary brands, and are ludicrously overpriced.

Carafe. Brand name of Gough Brothers for four French wines (including a dry and a medium white) which are of double-litre quality even though they only come in single-litre bottles.

Carafino. Brand name of Morgan Furze for three everyday wines sold through the Peter Dominic chain. The red and the white are Hungarian at the time of writing, the pink is Spanish. All three are reasonable both in quality and in price.

carbon dioxide. Formed during all stages of fermentation, this non-toxic gas is the agent responsible for the sparkle in sparkling wines, whatever their method of production.

Carema. ⋄ Val d'Aosta.

Carignan. The dominant red wine grape of the south of France. Not (yet) much used as a varietal name.

Carillon. Brand name of quite honest-tasting French ordinary wines made by Margnat and marketed by one of the oldest houses in the U.K., Christopher's. The red is full-bodied, the white and the pink both a little sweet. Available in ordinary and (cheaper) litre bottles.

Cariñena. The name commonly applied to all wines, red or white, produced in Aragon, in the region south of Zaragoza which more or less continues the Rioja southwards.

Casal Garcia. A Vinho Verde. The white comes in the familiar flat flask. The red, in an ordinary bottle, is never seen in England.

casa vinicola. (I) Winery.

Cassis. The unique position of the Cassis vineyards (limestone slopes just east of Marseille, facing south towards the sea which tempers the heat) has earned them one of the very few ACs of Provence. The white wine is very dry and fresh.

Castel Danielis. Brand name of Achaïa-Clauss for a dry dark table wine from the Peloponnese which some reckon to be the best red wine of all Greece.

Castella. Brand name of Victoria Wine & Tylers for three colours of cheap Spanish wine. When found at the Wine Market the double-litre bottles were an inexplicable 50 per cent dearer.

Castelli Romani. A district in the Alban hills, south-east of Rome, which produces white wines: firm dry pasta wines, nice abboccatos, and very good sweet ones. Paradoxically, what is marketed in England under this name is usually a cheap double-litre red, probably made from the dark Aleatico grapes, which would not be regarded very highly in its homeland.

Castelo Real. ⇨ Ribatejo.

Catalonia. The coastal region of Spain stretching south from Gerona is different from Castilian Spain not only in its language but also in the care it takes over its wines. The white Alella of its extreme north, sparkling Panadés of the middle, and even the dry reds of Priorato in the south can all compete quite happily with comparable wines of France.

cave. (F) Cellar.

Cawarra Claret. ⇨ Hunter Valley.

CB. On English wine lists: château-bottled.

cellar book. In a vineyard, this is the ledger in which origin, time of harvest and treatment of each wine are recorded. For private use, a cellar book can give a more or less detailed record of wines you have bought or drunk. The Wine Society sells a loose-leaf one for the price of a bottle. Using a page for each wine, you should (ideally) record name, region, grape, vineyard, year, shipper; date, place

and price of purchase, quantity bought; finally remarks on
your own tasting experience.

cellier. (F) Not a cellar, but an above-ground store for wine.

Cendré de Novembre. ⟡ vin gris.

cepa; cépage. (S; F) The species of grape or blend used for
making a particular wine.

Cépage Sauvignon. An increasingly familiar label for the
lesser wines of the Loire Atlantique. I find them preferable
to anything made from the Gros–Plant, and often also to the
more indifferent versions of Muscadet of the same region.

cépages nobles. (F) The official designation in Alsace for
the six best grape varieties used there. Generally, the
'noble' grape of a region is simply the one specified to
dominate its AC wines.

Cérons. A wine district along the left bank of the Garonne,
downstream from Barsac, which makes the same sweet
white wines as its neighbour but at more modest prices.

Chablis. A small town in the narrow valley of the river
Serein not far from its confluence with the Yonne. The
limestone and chalk hills of both banks produce what is
probably the most famous dry white wine in the world. The
seven grands crus are on the north bank (that is, facing
south) as are the best of the other vineyards. The Chardonnay grape here produces a green–tinged crisp and dry wine
with a distinctive but indescribable flavour. This is the
northernmost great wine in France, and spring frosts can
be severe. Quality varies greatly from year to year, and
sometimes even the good vineyards get no further than
characterless Petit Chablis, the AC for the lesser wines
which need only have 9·5 per cent alcohol compared with
10 for Chablis, 10·5 for the premiers crus and 11 for the
grands crus. With every step the depth and intensity of
colour, scent and flavour increase proportionally. So does
the price.

chai. (F) Store, sometimes wine-making plant, attached to a vineyard.

Chalonnais. ⇨ Côte Chalonnaise.

Chambéry. ⇨ vermouth.

Chambolle-Musigny. Very fine, slightly soft and delicately scented red wine from the middle of the Côte de Nuits.

chambrer. (F) To bring a wine to room temperature before use. The right thing to do with most full-bodied red wines, but not at all necessary for the lighter and younger ones. In any case, it is better to use the wine too cold (patience will remedy that soon enough) than to speed the process by dunking the bottle in hot water. On really indifferent wine, which you fear may be too harsh when cold, use tepid running water along the bottle for perhaps five minutes.

Champagne. Sparkling wine made in the Champagne district by a process known as the méthode champenoise. The producing area centres on Épernay and lies roughly between the Aube in the south, Reims in the north, Château Thierry in the west and Châlons-sur-Marne. The northern part, the Montagne de Reims, is planted with Pinot Noir; the south, especially the Côte des Blancs just below Épernay, grows the white Chardonnay. Champagnes are made from blends of these, in varying proportions resulting in varying character. Not too much need be said about them here, since no drinkable Champagne comes within our budget. With some diligence, however, it will at least be possible to buy decent half bottles at our price, in auctions or as bin ends. For most occasions, a good sparkling Saumur or the better Spanish sparklers like Freixenet are much to be preferred to cheap Champagne.

chaptalisation. The addition of sugar to the must with a view to increasing the eventual alcohol content of the wine. Widely practised in Germany, permitted for some wines in France, forbidden completely in Italy, it is everywhere subject to strict controls because one of the criteria for AC designation is the natural alcohol content of the wine. Jean-Antoine Chaptal was Napoleon's Minister of Agriculture, anxious to promote the use of beet sugar.

character. The specific properties of a wine which depend on the vineyard (soil, climate), the grape used, the processing and other factors. Eventually you learn to distinguish at least some of the characteristics even of the most everyday wines – in practical terms: you develop likes and dislikes.

Chardonnay. The grape which gives us all the best white Burgundies and is an important ingredient of Champagne is small, golden-yellow and very juicy. Even in California it produces wines of distinction.

Chassagne-Montrachet. At the southern end of the Côte de Beaune, Chassagne-Montrachet shares the area's most famous vineyards (Le Montrachet and Bâtard-Montrachet) with its northern neighbour, Puligny-Montrachet. Even the 'ordinary' white wines here are among the best of all France. The few reds are (by comparison) undistinguished.

Chasselas. White grape used extensively in Switzerland, both for the sparkling wines of Neuchâtel and the table wines of Valois (Fendant). In Germany it is often called Gutedel. In France it is but little used, Crépy and Pouilly-sur-Loire being its most notable wines.

Chassepré. Brand name of Nicolas for a very good medium-dry white blend.

Chasse-Spleen, Château. ⟡ Moulis.

château. (F) Estate. The château proper is merely the 'homestead' of the estate – seldom a 'castle' but often what in England is known as a 'country house', or a farm. Entries for specific châteaux will be found under the proper names.

Châteauneuf du Pape. Named after a fourteenth-century castle which is now only a ruin, this famous Rhône wine

is made of an astonishingly large number of different
grapes and consequently has a unique bouquet which needs
quite a while to develop: the better vintages are not at their
best inside ten years. Drunk young, like so many other
Rhône wines, it is rather harsh.

Chénas. One of the nine crus of Beaujolais, geographically
between Juliénas and Moulin à Vent. It is darker than the
latter, with which it shares the ability to age better than
most Beaujolais. It tends to be rather overpriced these days.

Chenin Blanc. ◊ Pineau de la Loire.

Chianti. The most popular Italian wine both at home and
abroad. Made in Tuscany from the Sangiovese grape,
mixed with 10 to 15 per cent white Malvasia and Trebbiano,
it comes in two versions. One is to be drunk young: this
one is made by the governo system and put in flasks. The
other is often aged in the wood for as much as five years
and then ages (and keeps) remarkably well in ordinary
bottles. Ricasoli is the great name in Chiantis, and Brolio
is the best of the long-lived Ricasolis.

Chianti classico is a vigorously controlled name now,
which can be given only to wines from the precisely defined heartland of Tuscany, south of Florence and north of
Siena. 'White Chianti' is no longer a lawful name.

Chile. This country has long produced the best wines of
South America, as well as the widest range. Its two
thousand miles of vineyards, mostly on volcanic soils, slope
away from the Andes mountains towards the Pacific. They
all get plenty of sun, but the amount of rain differs dramatically. In the far south the vines drown, the extreme north
gets no rain at all. The large middle region of which
Santiago is the centre has an ideal climate and grows the
main Bordeaux grapes, Bordeaux-fashion. The Cabernet
especially, if handled carefully, gives results which are
'perhaps the greatest wine bargain anywhere' (Hugh

Johnson, *World Atlas of Wine*, page 235). So far, we are not being given much chance to avail ourselves of this bargain: I have found only one 'Cabernet: Chilean red wine' for sale here. It is soft, pleasant, and altogether honest.

China. Traditional Chinese wines are made from rice, not from grapes. Recently, some grape-wines started appearing on the export market. The very few I have seen in the U.K. all seem to come from the Tsingtao Winery: Ch'ing-tao is the port of the Shantung peninsula, on the same latitude as Sicily. All are labelled simply 'dry red', 'dry white' or 'sparkling' by the rather ominously named National Cereal Oil and Foodstuffs Import and Export Company. Not at all bad wines (especially the white), but not worth their rather high price. Beware: the Kung Fu brand of 'Chinese style' wines comes from Spain.

Chinon. Red wine of the Loire, much admired by Rabelais who was born in the region, but largely ignored by the English and (even if at the top end of our range) still underpriced. Made from pure Cabernet Franc, the wine has a wild raspberry smell. It keeps well, but like most Loire reds is usually drunk young, and cool. Chinon itself is on the Vienne, a small tributary cutting deeply into chalk ground riddled with caves, some of which are used for ageing the wine.

Chiqua, La. Another unfortunate brand name for Spanish wines. This one covers the second rank marketed by Mackinlay-McPherson (Edinburgh) whose Santiago is considerably better, at only a few pence more. 'Restaurateurs find the five-gallon containers particularly useful', unfortunately. The whole lot came rock bottom in a *Which?* test many years ago, but that seems to have made little impact.

Chiroubles. One of the nine crus of Beaujolais, light and fruity.

Choix du Roy. Brand name of Balls Brothers for four cheap
wines bottled in France and apparently produced in the
Rhône region: a fruity red, sweet and medium whites, and
a fresh pink. They sell in litre and two-litre bottles – no
saving in buying the larger one.

Chorey-lès-Beaune. ⋄ Côte de Beaune-Villages.

Christian Brothers. A very successful wine-producing
operation in the hills of the south-western Napa Valley,
founded in 1882 by the Brothers of the Christian Schools
and still run by them to finance their novitiate at Mount La
Salle. Their wines are known, as usual in California, by
varietal names only. The whole range of reds is available
here (Cabernet Sauvignon, Gamay Noir, Pinot Noir and a
good Zinfandel) as well as the very pleasant Chenin Blanc.

Cissac. A small parish just above the most famous part of
Saint-Estèphe in the Haut-Médoc. The soil is different
here, the red wine less strong and deep but reliable all the
same and (like a lot of the 'ordinary' wines of the Médoc)
often very good value for not too much money.

Citran, Château. ⋄ Avensan.

clairet. (F) Pink wine. ⋄ also Auberge.

Clairette. Grape which is responsible for some of the best
white wines of southern France: it can take more sun than
most. Clairette du Languedoc is a strong, dry wine from
the Hérault which to gain its AC must be made solely
from the grape it is named after.

   Clairette de Die is a different thing altogether: a fruity
semi-sparkler.

claret. Name by which the (formerly very light) red wines
of Bordeaux have been known in England ever since the
region was acquired through the marriage of Henry II
and Eleanor of Aquitaine in 1152. The word carries no
legal obligations, and clarets or 'claret-style' wines from
other regions abound at the lower end of the market. In

America and Australia, especially, the term is used for any dry, medium-bodied red table wine.

classed growth. ◊ cru.

classico. (I) Epithet officially applied only to the wine from the central (best) area of its region, e.g. Chianti classico. Unofficially, it now gives rise to such delightful absurdities as 'classico vino da pasto'.

climat. (F) Vineyard. Used mostly in Burgundy.

climate. The influence of the weather during the hundred days after flowering is crucial to the character of the eventual wine. Initially, a certain amount of moisture is essential, but once the fruit has set, drier weather is needed so that the nourishing elements of the soil are not doo diluted. During the ripening period, from early August, warm bright sunshine is required. Before the harvest a certain amount of moisture is necessary again, to allow the ferments to form on the outside of the skins. Ideal conditions are somewhat hard to come by, and no two years are ever the same.

clos. (F) An individual vineyard. Used mostly for the smaller properties of Burgundy.

Clos de Vougeot. ◊ Burgundy.

Clos l'Église. Clos René. ◊ Pomerol.

Clotte, Château la. ◊ Saint-Émilion.

colheita. (P) Vintage.

collage. (F) ◊ fining.

College. Brand name of a good range of medium-priced wines marketed by Dolamore (London, but with branches in Oxford and Cambridge – hence the name). All five are bottled 'in their district of origin', but what that is, is not always easy to determine. There are two reds, Claret and Gamay, and three whites: Demi-sec, Blanc de Blancs and Hock. The Gamay and the Blanc I could drink for a long time.

Colli Albani. Horace said that the Alban Hills wine was excellent when nine years old; Pliny liked it even older.

Nowadays, the white wine marketed under this name is an undistinguished but drinkable pasta wine, lighter than the Frascati from the same region (probably because it is made from only two of the regional grapes, Trebbiano and Malvasia) and very young indeed.

colour. The colour of a wine depends on the pigments of the tannin present in the grape skins, and on the time these are left with the fermenting must before racking.

Commandaria. 'The wine of the Crusaders', and it must have fortified them greatly, for it is about the sweetest broth in Christendom. Named after the Grande Commanderie established on Cyprus by the Knights Templar in the twelfth century, it has retained its reputation but rarely its quality. If you find it within the price range of this guide, it will be a factory-made dessert wine not nearly as sweet as its formidable traditional namesake, and quite without any character whatsoever.

commune. (F) Parish; but can also mean an association of local growers.

Condrieu. Just downstream from the Côte Rôtie are the remarkably sheltered vineyards of Condrieu, which make equally remarkable white wines from a local grape called Viognier.

consorzio. (I) Association of local growers, recognized by law and active in protecting the standards and defining the exact limits of a producing area.

Coonawarra. ⬧ Australia.

Corbières. The large area of limestone hills south-east of Carcassonne and south-west of Narbonne in the Aude department (but in the Languedoc in wine terms) produces robust, not to say rough red wines which are being improved steadily by new production methods. Most of them are of VDQS standard, either as Corbières or Corbières du Roussillon (farther south towards Perpignan), but some already merit the AC Fitou. Château Pech Vermeil even releases vintage wines which are very good. The region also produces the traditional Clairette whites and Grenache pinks.

Cornas. An area on the right bank of the Rhône between Hermitage and Valence (both on the left bank) which makes good, strong red wines. They have neither the character nor the life-span of their northern cousins, but are excellent table wines all the same.

Corrida. Unfortunate brand name used by Stowell's of Chelsea for Spanish carafe wines made by the more interestingly named Compañia de los Vinos Generosos. A byword for anyone who wants to sum up his dislike of cheap plonk, and not without reason. The pink, however, is as honest as any you drink (and adore) on holiday.

Corsica. The one French island in the Mediterranean produces fairly indifferent wines dominated, as in Provence, by the pinks. They have recently been considered good enough to merit an AC – Vin de Corse – which on the whole is better taken as a warning rather than a recommendation.

Corvo. Good Sicilian wine made in two varieties, a straw-coloured white with a distinctive and full flavour, and a full-bodied rather aromatic red which is quite dry but hints of a hidden sweetness.

cosecha. (S) Vintage.

Costières du Gard. The right bank of the Rhône between Beaucaire and Vauvert. Its gravelly soil and hot climate produce rich, full-bodied VDQS reds from Syrah and other grapes, and equally strong whites from the Clairette.

côte. (F) Hillside vineyard. Hence Côte(s) de ... as the appellation for larger regions composed of such vineyards as opposed to those of river valleys and other flatlands, which are usually inferior.

coteaux. (F) Although technically the same as côte(s), this diminutive always denotes wine of VDQS rather than AC standards.

Coteaux d'Aix-en-Provence. General name for all ordinary wines from the region which live up to VDQS standards, slightly higher for reds than for the others. Some of it is better known under brand names like Lou Picassou.

Coteaux de Carthage. ♢ Tunisia.

Coteaux de Ksará. ♢ Lebanon.

Coteaux de la Loire. An AC for Muscadets from a region just upstream from Nantes. Anjou-Coteaux de la Loire can only be applied to the better Cabernet rosés of Anjou.

Coteaux du Languedoc. Thirteen red and pink wines from the scattered Hérault communes have the right to this VDQS designation. Some have become well known under their proper place names, especially those of the saints Christol, Drézéry and Georges around Montpellier. All are excellent everyday wines, of no great individual character or distinction. Saint-Chinian now has its own appellation.

Coteaux du Layon. The lower part of the Layon valley (which reaches the Loire at Chalonnes) produces the largest quantity and the best of the pinks marketed as Rosé d'Anjou and Cabernet d'Anjou. The region deserves more credit for its very individual but always golden, fragrant and full white wines made from the Pineau de la Loire. Bonnezaux and Quarts de Chaume are thought to be the best of these and have ACs of their own.

Côte Chalonnaise. The southward extension of the Côte d'Or vineyards takes its name from the market town Chalon-sur-Saône, halfway between Dijon and Mâcon but nowhere near the vineyards. The northern stretch is easily the better, especially the neighbouring villages of Rully, Mercurey and Givry. The authorized grapes are the Chardonnay for whites and Pinot Noir for reds.

Côte de Beaune. Name for the Burgundy vineyards stretch-

48

ing down from Beaune to the south-west. Also, the AC for the ordinary wines of this area, where bad wines seem to be impossible to make. These ordinary ones do, however, mature more quickly than their grander cousins.

Côte de Beaune-Villages. The AC for red wines from the better communes among the Côte de Beaune vineyards. Several of the contributing villages also have a right to their own AC. Among the ones not listed separately in this guide are Chorey-lès-Beaune and Pernand-Vergelesses. Their wines may not be special by Burgundy standards, but that only shows that the Burgundy standards themselves are rather special.

Côte de Brouilly. Mountain slopes with granite soil produce fine dark-purple wines in the middle of the more common Brouilly area. Of high alcohol content, they age well but, in common with most other Beaujolais, seldom get a chance to.

Côte de Nuits. A name without official status for the wine-producing region around Nuits-Saint-Georges.

Côte de Nuits-Villages. The AC for the wine of five small villages at the northern end of the Côte de Nuits. They all have a right to use their own name separately as well, but only Fixin seems ever to be heard of.

Côte de Provence. This Mediterranean coastal region between Marseille and Nice produces a large number of VDQS wines, of which the full, dry and fruity rosés are the best known.

Côte des Blancs. ♢ Champagne.

Côte d'Or. Collective name for an area discussed under the names of its two component parts, Côte de Nuits and Côte de Beaune.

Côte Rôtie. The most northern AC area of the Rhône vineyard makes exceptionally good red wines from the dark Syrah or Hermitage grape. They have a slight raspberry flavour, improve greatly with more age than they are usually given, and are still much underpriced compared with Burgundies or good clarets.

Côtes d'Auvergne. The lower hills of the Massif Central below Clermont-Ferrand produce indifferent wine of all colours barely meriting their VDQS. I have not seen any in the U.K. yet, but it is precisely from this kind of untapped well that one can expect the worst in years to come.

Côtes de Blaye. A fairly large wine-producing area touching the right bank of the Gironde at Blaye and running some twenty-five kilometres inland. A very small part of it, south of Blaye, continues the Côtes de Bourg and makes similar red wines which use the appellation Premières Côtes de Blaye. The bulk of wine from the Blayais is white, however. Dry, crisp and rather full, most of it is everyday wine of no particular distinction except for being fairly cheap.

Côtes de Bourg. A small wine region on the left bank of Dordogne and Gironde, right opposite Margaux. It makes mostly red wines, for which like the Médoc it uses Cabernet grapes. They probably age well, but are sold and therefore mostly drunk very young indeed, about two years after the vintage. Châteaux de Barbe and Rousselle, both at Villeneuve near the river, Les Richards in the hills near Mombier, and scores of others produce reliable if a little thin wines which form the cheap end of claret.

Côtes de Buzet. Between the Garonne (just below Agen) and the Baise lies a stretch of vineyards which produce rather full reds much like minor clarets, and good dry whites. Both are still underestimated and (if you can find them at all) underpriced.

Côtes de Duras. The northern tip of the Lot-et-Garonne département can be seen either as an eastern extension of the Entre-deux-mers area or as a south-western extension of Bergerac. Its red and white wines reflect this dilemma, but on the whole tend towards minor clarets.

Côtes de Fronsac. The wines of this hill region east of the river l'Isle form a second rank to those of Canon-Fronsac farther towards the Dordogne. They are relatively cheap, and can be drunk relatively young.

Côtes de Montravel. ⇨ Montravel.

Côtes du Luberon. Decent enough red wine of VDQS status, from the Rhône region in wine terms or southern Vaucluse in administrative terms. Resembles Provençal wines rather than Rhônes.

Côtes du Rhône. The banks of the Rhône between Vienne and Avignon produce a number of very different wines from a variety of grapes dominated by Syrah, Grenache and Clairette. From the left bank come the great red wines of Hermitage, Châteauneuf du Pape, Gigondas; from the right bank the rosés of Tavel and Lirac. Wine sold under the sole name Côtes du Rhône now mostly comes from the southern regions of Vaucluse and Gard, but some of the wines from these neglected areas are at last gaining friends for their own individual merit. Costières du Gard is the VDQS for some very good everyday wine, and Côtes du Ventoux was elevated from VDQS to AC status in 1973.

Côtes du Rhône-Villages. The AC for fourteen communes in the southern part of the Rhône vineyard which make dependable red wines of no great individual character. Each village has the right to hyphenate its own name to the Côtes du Rhône epithet, but only Vacqueyras seems to do this with any consistency.

Côtes du Roussillon. The area between the rivers Têt and Tech, south of Perpignan, makes rather strong wines of all colours which have the right to this AC or to the slightly higher-rated one of Côtes du Roussillon-Villages.

Côtes du Ventoux. The slopes of the Ventoux mountain, rising out of the coastal plains of the Rhône as a first indication of the highlands to come, produce attractive Syrah red and some pink and white wines which have not only gained AC rights recently but are also fast establishing themselves on the U.K. market as very good Côtes du Rhône wines at most attractive prices.

Coufran, Château. ◊ Saint-Seurin-de-Cadourne.

coupage. (F) Blending.

Couronne, Château la. ◊ Pauillac.

Cramant. Virtually the only Champagne village to market its wine under its own name. Just south of Épernay in the Côte des Blancs, it is known for its Blancs de Blancs: a fully-fledged Champagne and a half-sparkling (crémant) one. They are very light and delicate compared with the blended Champagnes.

cream. Very sweet and often darkish: used only of sherry. Bristol Cream is a registered trademark of Harvey's, but Bristol Milk is not.

crémant. (F) 'Creaming', denotes slightly sparkling wines.

Crépy. The dry, crisp, light white wine from this Savoy village could easily be confused with most Swiss Fendant wines, for the simple reason that it comes from the same region (the shores of Geneva Lake) and is made from the same grape.

criadera. ◊ solera.

criado por ... (S) Grown by ...

Criolla. ◊ Argentina; Franchette.

Crozes-Hermitage. Lesser relatives of the famous Hermitage, grown in the neighbouring Côtes du Rhône vineyards. The reds are also made from the Syrah grape but do not keep as long as Hermitage itself.

cru. (F) A specific vineyard, also the wine which is grown there – hence the English version as 'growth'. The term 'classed growth' derives from the division into different classes of excellence long practised in the Médoc (◊ cru classé) and extended to other areas.

cru artisan. (F) In the Médoc, the class below cru bourgeois.

cru bourgeois. (F) The class of Bordeaux wines below the crus classés. In the Médoc alone, distinction is made between cru bourgeois supérieur and the more ordinary cru bourgeois. Often such distinctions lie in a 1 per cent difference in alcohol content.

cru classé. (F) Usually, any classed growth. The Médoc alone subdivides its wines officially into five numbered classes – what Cyril Ray in his book *The Wines of France* calls the peerage: 'Lafite and the other first growths are dukes; Léoville Barton, for example, a marquess; Palmer an earl; Beychevelle a viscount; Cantemerle a baron'. There are only sixty-two of these, among a roll-call of over a thousand clarets which make do with the lower ranks of cru exceptionnel, cru bourgeois supérieur, cru bourgeois, cru artisan and cru paysan, in this descending order. This hierarchy, first formulated over a century ago, has become the basis for similar systems in other regions, with modifications to suit regional needs. Other Bordeaux areas, for instance, use two instead of five classes for their top wine (grand cru precedes premier cru).

cru exceptionnel. (F) In the Médoc, the class that comes below the five groups of crus classés. Being above cru bourgeois supérieur, it is a sort of upper middle class. True to the letter of its epithet, it is conferred but rarely.

cru paysan. (F) In the Médoc, the class below cru artisan: the bottom rung of the ladder.

crusted. Non-vintage port, bottled early, and sometimes labelled 'vintage character'. The name derives from the crust formed during the ageing process on the inside face of the bottle by salts of tartaric acid.

Cussac. Upstream from Saint-Julien, the Cussac area is the beginning of the 'poor' central part of the Haut-Médoc. No classed growth, no outstanding wines for the connoisseur, the wine-writer or the merchant to wax lyrical and pricey – but a large stream of solid drinking wine at prices rather more within our range than most. Similar wines are produced in the neighbouring parishes of Saint-Laurent, inland to the north-west, and Lamarque, upstream. Château de Lamarque is a good example of the bright red wines of the area, which can be drunk quite young.

cuve close. (F) Method of producing sparkling wine in which the necessary second fermentation takes place in bulk in closed vats instead of individually in the bottle (as in the méthode champenoise). Known in the U.S. as 'bulk process'.

cuvée. (F) Blend. Used mostly of Champagne.

Cuvée Sérain. Brand name of Balls Brothers for a Chablis.

Cyprus. One of the oldest wine-producing regions anywhere, and the first part of the Islamic world to bring its viticulture back to important proportions. The vineyards are concentrated in the (Greek) south-western part of the island, high on the slopes of the Troodos mountains. Cyprus never had phylloxera, and still uses mostly native vines like the Mavron ('black') and the Xynisteri. Its most famous wine is Commandaria, but the bulk of its produce (and 80 per cent of its exports) has long consisted of sherry-type wines of very inferior quality. Only recently, with the introduction of the proper Spanish production methods, has the island started to make 'real' sherry. Of the table wines, the red Othello and the white Aphrodite are the best known in the U.K. A great deal of the wine production is handled by combines large enough to afford advanced modern processing methods. Most of these, like KEO, Kolossi and SODAP, are based on Limassol, the main port of the area.

D

Dão. The Dão is a sheltered region in the centre of Portugal, between the Estrela and Caramulo mountains. One of the regiãos demarcadas, it produces strong ruby-red wines with a surprisingly smooth taste, and pale yellow whites which are light and aromatic but should be drunk as young as possible. The reds are often found in the U.K., at widely differing prices which do not necessarily reflect similar differences in quality. They would probably age quite well, but are seldom given a chance.

decanting. A good practice with older wines, especially those with a sediment. Pour the wine very slowly into the decanter, holding the bottle against some source of light in such a way that you can look through the neck clearly: this will show just when sediment starts to make its way out (at which point, stop pouring). Wines drunk rather too young often benefit from the dash of oxygen given by decanting them, and cheap artificially sweetened wines, held in equilibrium in the bottle by sulphur dioxide, get a chance to lose their evil-smelling sulphur.

De Georges. Monsieur and Madame, Comte and Comtesse, Marquis and Marquise, Duc and Duchesse, Prince and Princesse – the De Georges dynasty is surprisingly large, works on the rather twee principle that the females are white and the males red, comprises French wines from a variety of regions mostly under A C labels, and is 'shipped and bottled by De Tenet & De Georges, Bordeaux &

Nuits St Georges, for Tesco Stores Ltd'. The AC wines
will be up to reasonable standards, about the few others I
am not so sure. 'Fine old claret' covers a Cabernet which
could just as well be Chilean and cannot have been in
anybody's bottle longer than four years. 'Gamay de France'
tastes, predictably enough, like a Beaujolais, but a very thin
one. No store seems to carry the full range, and by the
end of 1975 some stocks were still at 'pre-budget' prices.
The current prices are not exactly low – the Chénas
especially is much too expensive.

Deidesheim. The first important centre of the Mittelhaardt.
Under the new classification most of its many individual
vineyard names have disappeared, but all of them were
among the best wines of the region, Riesling whites of
great distinction.

delicate. Light, and with a good but easily disturbed balance.

Demestica. Name of a light red wine, and a pleasantly
fragrant dry white one, from the Peloponnese. Both are
marketed by Achaïa-Clauss, one of the largest wine producers of Greece, with headquarters in Patras.

demi-sec. (F) Medium dry, except when applied to Champagne: then it means sweetish.

denominação de origem. (P) Guarantee of origin, similar
to AC status.

denominación de origen. (S) Guarantee of origin, similar
to AC status, administered by a Consejo Regulador for
each individual region.

denominazione di origine controllata. (I) Guarantee that
the wine comes from a specified vineyard and that this
vineyard's production is controlled by law. Again similar
to the French appellation system.

denominazione di origine controllata e garantita. (I) An
extension of the foregoing, used only for high-quality wine
and in current practice almost confined to the best Chiantis.

denominazione semplice. (I) Guarantee that the wine is made from the traditional grapes of a specified region. In status similar to VDQS.

dessert wine. Descriptive term covering all sweetish or really sweet wines which taste better with the pudding than the main course, but which are quite often excellent on their own, like port or Tokay.

Deutsche Weinstrasse. The long string of vineyards of the Rheinpfalz.

Dhron. A small village situated where the river Dhron joins the Moselle. It makes a large quantity of sound white wine of no great distinction.

Dimiat. ⬧ Bulgaria.

Dingač. At the expensive end of the Yugoslav wine list, a very strong red from Dalmatia, with just a hint of sweetness.

Dingle's Plonk. ⬧ supermarkets.

DOC. ⬧ denominazione di origine controllata.

doce. (P) Sweet.

Doçura. Brand name of Gilbey Vintners for a light and fairly sweet Portuguese red.

dolce. (I) Sweet, usually very sweet.

Doluca. Firm which produces a large range of mostly white wines in northern Turkey. The single-grape ones are the best. The smooth red wine made from the native Papazkarasi should not be drunk less than ten years old; the Sémillon varieties also age well if not as spectacularly. The Riesling is all right, but the much cheaper mixes of Sémillon and Riesling are indifferent. The rosé, apparently made from Gamay grapes, I have never even seen. Doluca's better wines are sometimes labelled Villa Doluca.

Dom. A prefix to names on German wine labels which denotes that the wine stems from a vineyard belonging to the cathedral of Trier: as good a guarantee of quality as one can get.

Domaine d'Aliera

Domaine d'Aliera. ▷ KEO.

Dom Bazilio. Brand name for a range of Portuguese blended export wines, in characteristic wide and long-necked bottles. Both the red and the white come mainly from the Ribatejo region, the white being from Valada. The red has some Douro blended in, and the pink is mostly Douro.

Dominic, Peter. ▷ Carafino; wine-store chains.

Don Cortez. Brand name of Grants of St James's for a range of Spanish wines which were nice and reliable even in the days when they were called 'Spanish Sauternes' and other now equally illegal names. There are five different ones: a full-bodied red which has changed a lot since I drank it regularly but is still good; three whites including a good dry one from Toledo and a sweet wine I never had the courage to try; and a rosé I can live without. They all come in half bottles (as more cheap wine should, even if it is relatively dearer that way), in standard bottles and, cheapest of all, in litres.

double-litre wine. A term I use to avoid being abusive about the kind of ordinary wine which is cheap in every sense of the word and which really needs the economics of the large bottle (▷ price) to be put on the market at all. This in no way means to imply that all wine in large bottles is necessarily inferior.

doubles. ▷ magnum.

Douro. The most famous wine region of Portugal, steep river slopes of granite with a little soil (held in place by slate walls) producing the wines which blend into port. The lower part of the region grows red and white table wines of no particular merit, most of which go into blends with those of Dão. Many of the commoner pink wines come from this area, too, in an unreasonable variety of fancy bottles.

doux. (F) Sweet.

dry. Means no more than the opposite of sweet, and consequently varies with the kind of wine it is applied to: dry
Champagne, for instance, is quite sweet really, and a dry
Graves or a dry Chablis are worlds apart. For red wine the
word is hardly used at all except at the cheap end of the
market where so many of the heavier red wines are
sweetish.

Dürnstein. Name of a place and, more important, of a huge
growers' co-operative in the Wachau region of Austria.

dulce. (S and R) Sweet.

Durbach. ⟡ Baden.

duty. The duty levied by H.M. Customs & Excise on all
substances containing alcohol is the main reason why your
everyday wines are not as cheap as they could be. The
snag is that this duty is related to the percentage of alcohol,
not to the value of the product: you pay as much on plonk
as on Yquem. The present rates of duty are quite fierce:
still wines imported in bottle from Germany were already
taxed at £5 per case of twelve bottles, those coming from
France at £5.50, and the April 1976 budget added another
70p to these figures. For non-E.E.C. countries the rates are
even higher. The duty on sparkling wine is £7 per case,
which may be negligible in the case of a grand Champagne
but effectively doubles the price of a Saumur (⟡ price).

E

Edelzwicker. Name given to Alsatian wines made from a mixture of the region's cépages nobles.

Egri Bikavér. ♦ Bull's Blood.

Eigenbaugewächs. (G) An Austrian term for wine from the producer's own vineyard.

eigene Abfüllung. (G) Bottled by the producer.

eigenes Wachstum. (G) From the producer's own vineyard.

Einzellage. (G) Individual vineyard.

elaborado por . . . (S) Made by . . .

Elat. ♦ Israel.

Elba. ♦ Aleatico; Tuscany.

embotellado. (S) Bottled.

embotellado de origen. (S) Estate-bottled.

engarrafado. (P) Bottled.

engarrafado na origem. (P) Estate-bottled.

England. The medieval vineyards, some dating back to Roman days and recorded in the Domesday Book, usually belonged to the Church. They faded away owing to improving trade with France and seem to have disappeared even before the dissolution of the monasteries. In the early 1950s a few attempts were made to start wine production up again, and these attempts proved so successful that every year now sees the creation of several new vineyards, mostly in Suffolk and Sussex. A cross between Riesling and Sylvaner vines known as Müller-Thurgau is by far the most popular grape, but the newer Seyve-Villard may well replace it eventually. A complete list of private and commercial vineyards can be found in Gillian Pearkes: *Growing Grapes in Britain* (Andover, Amateur Winemaker Magazine, 1973).

The oldest commercial vineyard is Hambledon, started in 1952; the best-known is Pilton Manor, and the fastest-growing recent addition is Adgestone. As far as vintages have a meaning yet, 1975 would have been the best year ever for wine-making in this country, but for the autumn rains.

Entre-deux-mers. The two 'seas' are the rivers Garonne and Dordogne, and the region between them produces both red and white wine of greatly varying quality. What is commonly found under the simple name is an indifferent cheap white, good for little but spaghetti parties. The better white wines of the region come from the north bank of the Garonne and are labelled Premières Côtes de Bordeaux, the red ones having to make do with Bordeaux or Bordeaux Supérieur.

Erbach. This is the easternmost village in the Rheingau to produce wines of distinction. The large Marcobrunnen vineyards are the most famous, but generally all Erbach wines are among the best of the whole region.

espumante; espumoso. (P; S) Sparkling.

estate-bottled. Wine bottled at the place where the grapes were grown and processed.

Est est est. A nice dry white wine from Montefiascone and the Lake Bolsena region of the Lazio, north of Rome. It is made from Malvasia and Trebbiano grapes and derives its name from a rather spurious legend on a local gravestone.

étampé. (F) Of corks: branded with the name of producer or bottler.

extra dry, extra sec. Dry. Used only for Champagne.

Ezerjó. ⇨ Mór.

F

Faisca. Good semi-sparkling Portuguese wines, either white or pink, from Setúbal.

FB. On English wine lists: bottled in France, but not necessarily at the vineyard.

Federweisser. (G) Very young wine, bottled before the end of fermentation and drunk as soon as possible.

Felicidad. Brand name for some very indifferent Spanish wines not likely to inspire the feeling their name promises.

Fendant. One of the best Swiss wines, made at Sion in the Valais canton, on the Rhône, from Chasselas grapes (their local name is also Fendant). Bottled when only a few months old the wine often retains a slight sparkle.

fermentation. The chemical process by which the fructose in the must is transformed into alcohol and carbon dioxide, under the catalytic influence of ferments.

ferments. The yeasts that turn grape sugar into alcohol. They are formed on the skin of the ripe grape while it is still on the vine. The most important one is called *Saccharomyces ellipsoideus*.

Fetească. A native Romanian grape which is used in two varieties, the albă (white) and more often the regală. Its rather light white table wines are known by the grape name, often without so much as a region of origin being mentioned.

Figeac, Château. ♢ Saint-Émilion.

Finch's. ♢ Barrera; Pinson.

Fine Fare. The range of Spanish 'Burgundy', 'Sauternes'

and 'Chablis' which even the *Which?* report of 1970 rated dismally low seems to have disappeared, but the new La Mañana is of the same kind. For better wines on the Fine Fare shelves ⟡ Fleuron, for more unpleasantness ⟡ Santa Maria.

Finger Lakes. ⟡ U.S.A.

fining. Clarification of wine by means of protein substances which, with the natural tannin, bring down all unwanted particles clouding the wine. This 'collage' is a general practice, for which different regions use different sub- stances. Egg-white is used for the fine red wines of France, fish-glue (or more politely isinglass) for whites.

Fino. A light, pale and dry sherry.

Fitou. Five communes north of the Étang de Leucate, in- cluding Fitou and Leucate itself, and a few others much higher up in the Corbières hills, make red wines which have merited the AC Fitou rather than the very wide area VDQS Corbières. Rough when young, they mature quickly into smooth dark wines with a distinctive bouquet.

Fixin. ⟡ Côte de Nuits-Villages.

flat. Dull and uninteresting, usually because of very low acidity.

Fleurie. Probably the freshest and most fragrant of the Beau- jolais wines, best drunk young and even lightly chilled.

Fleurion. Brand name of French & Foreign Wines (London) for a very good white Burgundy from Chardonnay grapes.

Fleuron. A reasonably priced and quite ambitious range of AC wines from the various Bordeaux regions. The five whites are all sweet. The six reds come from the Médoc, the four Haut-Médoc districts and Pomerol – areas where badly made wine is hard to find. Marketed by Capital Wine & Travers (London), they are widely available through the Fine Fare chain, and seem more than equal to Tesco's similar if wider De Georges range.

flor. (S) A yeasty mould (*Mycoderma vini*) produced by fermentation. It affects sherries, Montilla and a very few other wines (like the vin jaune of the Jura) by covering the surface of the vat and shutting the 'working' wine off from the outside air. It is this process which gives these wines their distinctive taste.

Fontaine, La. Brand name of Casson Ltd (London) for three colours of cheap French 'table wine' of which the red is at least inoffensive while the rosé tastes of unidentifiable kernels rather than of the grape.

Forst. On the Deutsche Weinstrasse between Deidesheim and Wachenheim, this village's vineyards have the unique distinction of a dark, rich basalt soil which holds the sun's heat like a storage heater. Its wines are therefore richer and sweeter than other Rheinpfalz wines.

fortified wine. Wine which has had its alcohol content increased by the addition of grape spirit. Sherries are the most famous example.

foxy. A word often used to describe the characteristic taste of wines made from the Fox Vine, the native American *Vitis labrusca*. Easily recognized once experienced, but impossible to describe.

Fracia. ⟡ Valtellina.

France. Although at last overtaken by Italy in terms of quantity, it seems unlikely that France will ever be equalled in terms of quality and variety. No less than 9 per cent of the country's population is 'in wine' in one way or another, and the remainder is wine-conscious enough to consume 90 per cent of the product at home. The country actually imports more wine than it exports. Most exports come from the top end of the market, the 15 per cent that have the backing of the very strictly administrated appellations contrôlées. Lesser wines still have a second line of equally strict controls to contend with for the rank of 'vin délimité de qualité supérieure'.

French wine production is dominated by the reds which make up nearly three-quarters of the total. For further notes on the main wine regions see Alsace, Bordeaux, Burgundy, Côtes du Rhône, Languedoc, Loire and Provence.

Franchette. Brand name of Rigby & Evens (Cheshire) for a range of blended Argentinian wines imported in bulk. The red is better than the two whites, but the pink (which I did not find) might be worth trying. The Criolla grape from which it is made is native to Argentina and accounts for a large percentage of home consumption. Tesco Stores have taken up this line, which is also sold under the name Ruiz Belmonte.

Franken. The area along the meandering Main which has Würzburg as its centre and Nürnberg at its eastern end. It makes a characteristic dry but full-bodied white wine from Sylvaner grapes, grown on chalk or red marl and bottled in the Bocksbeutel flasks which are typical for the region. The most famous Frankenwein is Steinwein; other guarantees of quality are the names of two religious bodies with extensive holdings throughout the region: Bürgerspital and Juliusspital. Most is drunk very young, which is a waste for the best improve greatly with age.

Frankenwein. Popular rather than legal description of the better types of white wines from Franken, the ones traditionally bottled in Bocksbeutel flasks.

frappé. (F) 'Iced', that is: chilled; but not by dunking ice cubes into the wine.

Frascati. Fragrant, firm and remarkably golden in colour, this is the best white wine from the Lazio district known as the Castelli Romani. It is rather higher in alcohol content than most others in the region. The dry really is dry, and the abboccato very pleasantly sweet.

Freisa. A red wine made in the Piedmont between Turin and Asti from a local grape of the same name. At its best it is quite dry, with a characteristic raspberry flavour. There is a sweeter bubbly version which is a bit lemonade-like.

Freixenet. Sparkling wines from San Sadurní de Noya, in the Panadés region south-west of Barcelona. Made from three regional white grapes, Freixenets are true Blancs de Blancs made by the méthode champenoise. The 'Carta Nevada' variety comes in a frosted bottle which already looks cold. Although even the brut tastes slightly sweet to me, these cheap 'champagne' wines are excellent value.

French wine laws. ⬦ wine laws; for more specific information ⬦ appellation contrôlée and vin délimité de qualité supérieure.

Friuli. The extreme north-east of Italy, between Udine and Trieste, towards Yugoslavia. Most of its wines go under simple varietal names: red Merlot and Gamay, native white Tocai. The Pinot Grigio is coming into the area as well, having been used with success in the Alto Adige.

frizzante. (I) Half-sparkling.

Fronsac. ⬦ Canon-Fronsac; Côtes de Fronsac.

fructose. The natural sugar present in grapes and other fruit.

fruité. (F) Fruity.

fruity. Said of wine in which a certain amount of residual sugar retains the typical flavour of a specific variety of grape.

Fuder-Nr. (G) Cask number. Used only on Moselle labels, with reference to the 1,000-litre vats of the region.

Furmint. The great native white grape of Hungary, making some of the country's sweeter and more powerful wines like Tokay. It is widely used in the Balkan countries, too, and usually with pleasing and drier, if less spectacular, results.

G

Gaillac. One of the oldest wine-producing regions of France, on the banks of the Tarn, best known for its white wines which can be mousseux (by a unique local process) or just mildly perlant. The great variety in the taste of Gaillac wines is due to the soil: limestone on one bank, granite on the other.

Gamay. One of the most extensively used black grapes, named after a tiny village in the Côte de Beaune (where it is never used). It is high-yielding but produces a more ordinary wine than the Pinot Noir does. A mixture of the two is known as Passe-tout-grains.

The Gamay's best use is in the Mâconnais, Chalonnais and Beaujolais, where it thrives especially on granite soils. In California, too, it makes excellent wine, including pinks from a local variety called Napa Gamay to distinguish it from what the Americans call the Gamay Beaujolais. Its use in Friuli (northern Italy) is relatively new but very promising.

Gamza. A grape used in the Balkans, Bulgaria in particular, for clean red wines of strong flavour which go under the varietal name.

Gatão. One of the best of the Vinhos Verdes available in the U.K.

Gattinara. Made near the town of the same name, in the Po valley, from Nebbiolo grapes. With Barolo this is the best red wine of Piedmont, and consequently it is getting more expensive. Rich in tannin, it may appear somewhat harsh when young but matures well.

Gay-Lussac scale. Expression of alcohol content of a liquid in straight volume percentages, by means of the 'centesimal alcoholometer' for which Joseph Louis Gay-Lussac issued directives in 1824.

Gebiet. (G) A German wine-growing region, legally defined in the most general terms only (Moselle-Saar-Ruwer, for instance) and subdivided into more specific districts called Bereich.

Geisenheim. On the Rhine next to Rüdesheim, this village is perhaps more famous for its national wine college than for its actual produce. The latter is nevertheless on a par with the rest of the region, especially the many single-vineyard wines produced by the 'Staatliche Lehr- und Forschungsanstalt für Wein-, Obst- und Gartenbau' itself.

generic names. Wine names denoting a place of origin. The wider and vaguer of these names (Burgundy, Champagne) were often used to indicate that a wine from nowhere near these regions is supposed to have similar characteristics. The stricter international enforcement of wine laws has rid us of many of these: Champagne, for instance, is a protected name, while Burgundy is not.

generous. Descriptive term for wine with a high alcohol content.

Georgia. One of the larger and better wine-producing regions of the U.S.S.R. The vineyards are mostly at altitudes of 1,000 to 1,400 metres, on the southern slopes of the Caucasus mountains. They produce reliable, quite dry blended wines which are known by place-names and often, curiously, by numbers. Number 1 Tsinandali (with a hint of resin in its taste) and number 3 Gurdzhaani are quite good whites, number 4 Mukuzani is a very heavy red. Only these three are being imported here at present.

German wine laws. ⋄ wine laws; for more specific information ⋄ Qualitätswein (both entries).

Germany. German wine production is no more than a tenth

of the French, and native demand is such that only a small percentage is exported. Most of the wine produced, and nearly all that goes abroad, is white. The vineyards lie along the Rhine and its tributaries, and vary greatly in climate and soil. The variety of wines is equally great, but all the good ones have more flavour and a greater bouquet than the French whites outside Alsace. A delicate balance of sugar content against acidity is the cause of this, and the quality of German wines is officially determined by the must weight, not by the vineyard of origin: in theory, any vineyard could produce a top class wine. For the intricacies of present legislation see the two Qualitätswein entries.

The main wine-producing regions (Gebiete) are Ahr, Baden, Franken, Moselle-Saar-Ruwer, Nahe, Rheingau, Rheinhessen, Rheinpfalz and Württemberg. All of these will be found treated separately.

Gevrey-Chambertin. At the far northern end of the Côte de Nuits, this village has the unique distinction of continuing its vineyards right across the N74, the dreary road from Dijon to Beaune. Practically every last acre has the right to its own AC. The better ones hyphenate Chambertin after their own name, but even the simple place-name is an absolute guarantee of quality.

Gewürztraminer. Small, tightly packed white grape of a golden-yellow hue; spicy, fragrant and strong wines, often a little sweet. In Alsace it is one of the cépages nobles, second only to the Riesling. In Germany its use is confined to the south, especially Baden, but in Austria and the Tirol (both sides) it is used extensively, and in California its results are generally quite good.

Gigondas. One of the best of the less well-known Rhône wine areas, between Orange and the Côtes du Ventoux. Its red wine especially is of great character, deep in colour, powerful but pleasant. The rosés are all right when young.

Gilbey Vintners. ⋄ Doçura; Justina; Vista.

Givry. The true Pinot Noir red made in the Chalonnais hills around Givry can stand comparison with most Côte de Beaune, and in price it compares more than favourably. The whites are good, too, but not yet much known.

Goldener Oktober. A brand name which in the last ten years has captured a fair percentage of the German market and now apparently does quite well in the U.K. There are four varieties available here: a very indifferent sweet Liebfraumilch, a good Moselle-Saar-Ruwer (bound to vary from time to time, with a name like that covering all eventualities), a rosé and a pleasant Riesling. Imported by Grants of St James's and sold through another Allied Brewers subsidiary, the Victoria Wine chain.

Gospodaniile Agricole de Stat. The Romanian state agricultural and wine-producing co-operative.

Gough Brothers. ⋄ Carafe; Vin Gough.

goût américain. (F) On a Champagne label this means the wine is sweet indeed. One of the few instances where 'goût américain' and 'goût français' mean the same thing.

governo system. The provocation of malolactic fermentation to make a very rough wine more supple. It is done by adding a rich must to the wine after the first fermentation. As 'governo all'uso toscano' the process used to be typical for Tuscany and its Chianti production, but its use is spreading to other parts of Italy.

Graach. Downstream from Bernkastel, on the same bank, Graach continues the most important area of the Middle Moselle. Its beautiful white wines, especially the Spätleses which are sweetish even by German standards, age remarkably well and become really smooth. Himmelreich and Münzlay are the most famous vineyards, but the lesser (and less expensive) ones are all worth a try.

gradi (alcool). (I) Percentage of alcohol, by volume.

Gran Caruso. ⟡ Ravello.

grand cru. (F) A top growth in Burgundy which could carry
its own A C and rank above premier cru. ⟡ grand vin.

grand cru classé. (F) The second rank of Saint-Émilion
wines, following 'premier grand cru classé'.

Grandes-Murailles, Château. ⟡ Saint-Émilion.

grand vin. (F) Literally 'great wine', a term without moral or
legal obligation except in Alsace where grand vin or grand
cru denotes a wine with more than 11 per cent alcohol.

Grants of St James's. ⟡ Don Cortez; Goldener Oktober;
Sansovino; wine-store chains.

Graves. The left bank of the Garonne, from Langon down
to Bordeaux, takes its name from the soil, a gravelly sand
washed up by the river. The vineyards here are surrounded
by forest, and although the region is known for its white
wines the top stretch, nearest Bordeaux, makes only fine
reds which account for about a quarter of the total Graves
output. They correspond closely to those of the Haut-
Médoc on the other side of the city. Farther south, the
Léognan and Martillac communes make both reds and
whites of quality, and from there on it really is whites only.
These are dry and fragrant in the northern part, and tend to
get sweeter as the vineyards get closer to Sauternes. The
appellation Graves covers both red and white wines, but
Graves Supérieur is exclusively for whites with a degree
more alcohol.

Graves de Vayres. A small region in the north of the Entre-
deux-mers district, around the village of Vayres on the
Dordogne. It produces the best white wines of the district
and has long had its own A C.

Greece. Virtually the whole of the country, up to a height
of about a thousand metres, grows vines and makes wine.
Commercially, the Peloponnese takes the larger share. Its
sweet red Mavrodaphne and dry red or white Demestica

are well known even in the U.K. The most famous (or infamous, depending on your taste) Greek wine, Retsina, originates on the mainland. The islands of Samos and Rhodes specialize in sweet wines, the latter in a Malvasia or Malmsey. Few, if any, Greek wines rise above the level of sound table wines. The names of the bigger manufacturers (Achaïa-Clauss, Metaxas and Cambas) guarantee a fairly consistent standard.

Grenache. A sweet black grape which grows in large tight bunches and is used mostly for the better pink wines, from the Rhône to California where it occupies the highest acreage after the Zinfandel but where most of its wine is used for blending. Only in Spain does it make good red wines.

Grignolino. A light red wine from the Asti region of Piedmont, made from local grapes of the same name and usually drunk cool and quite young.

Gris. ⟡ vin gris.

Grk. A beautiful, very dry 'white' wine (its colour really is remarkably dark) made on the islands off the Dalmatian coast of Yugoslavia, especially Korčula.

Grombalia. ⟡ Tunisia.

Gros-Plant. One of the oldest native grapes used along the lower Loire. Its white wine, known as Gros-Plant du Pays Nantais, is a VDQS of low alcohol content, almost no colour and even less taste.

Grosslage. (G) A group of vineyards called by the name of the best known among them. Common practice after the last changes in the German wine laws.

growth. ⟡ cru.

Grumello. ⟡ Valtellina.

Guntersblum. Small village in the southern part of Rheinhessen.

Gurdzhaani. ⟡ Georgia.

Gutedel. German name for the Chasselas grape.

H

Hallgarten. One of the wine villages of the Rheingau which are away from the river, in the hills. Its vineyards continue those of the Steinberg in neighbouring Hattenheim. They produce wine of the general high Rheingau standard.

Hambledon. Established in 1952, this Hampshire vineyard is the oldest commercial one in England. It uses mostly Müller-Thurgau and Seyve-Villard vines. Its wine is available through The Wine Society.

hard. Describes a very dry (usually red) wine, with too much acidity.

harsh. Like astringent, this is said of a wine with too much tannin.

Hattenheim. The vineyards of this Rheingau town continue those of Erbach farther west along the river towards Oestrich. Their wines are good and dependable, especially those of the Steinberg vineyard.

Haut-Médoc. The best part of the Médoc vineyard, and the one which includes all the crus classés. Notes on the various communes it consists of will (in order of descent down the river) be found under Macau, Margaux, Moulis, Cussac, Saint-Julien, Pauillac, Saint-Sauveur, Cissac, Saint-Estèphe and Saint-Seurin.

heady. Said of a wine with a higher alcohol content than its taste leads one to suspect.

hectare. A measure for land areas commonly used to express vineyard sizes. One hectare is equivalent to 100 ares or 2·47 acres.

hectolitre. The liquid measure most commonly used to express wine production quantities. A hectolitre is equivalent to 22 imperial gallons or 26·4 American gallons.

Hérault. This large département of France, running south from the Garrigues hills to the Mediterranean coast between Narbonne and Aigues-Mortes, is not officially a wine district (in wine terms it is part of the Languedoc-Roussillon) but it does produce more wine than any other region all the same. Much of it is good VDQS ordinaries sold under the Coteaux du Languedoc label.

Hermitage. Although this vineyard on the high left bank well above Valence is perhaps the most famous of all the Rhône vineyards its wine is, paradoxically, much under-estimated. If it weren't, it would be at least twice the price, and it would not be drunk too young either, for this deep-purple, strong-flavoured, warm wine made solely from the Syrah grape needs a good ten years in the bottle before it is anywhere near its best.

Hermitage. ⟡ Syrah; Ugni Blanc.

Hirondelle. Brand name of Hedges & Butler (London) for a small group of table wines much sold by the glass in pubs. They change from time to time, are never bad but always indifferent. The *Which?* report of 1970 had them down as Austrian; they have also been 'general East European'. At the time of writing all are Italian, the white good and really dry, the red very thin and just a bit sweet.

Hochheim. The only vineyards of the Rheingau which are on flat 'palus' ground. Being out of the main wine area by a good fifteen miles, their wines are reckoned to 'belong' only because they have the same characteristic fullness and bouquet. It is from Hochheimer that the English first mispronounced 'Hock'.

hock. First recorded in 1625, this is an abbreviation of hockamore which in turn seems to have been the English pronunciation of Hochheimer. This word referred originally to the wines of Franken which were sent down the Main to be shipped abroad with other Rhine traffic from Hochheim. By extension it came to refer to Rhine wines.

The habit of drinking 'hocks' young is very recent indeed, and in the eighteenth and nineteenth centuries fine old hock was a highly prized (and priced) possession.

Hungary. The largest wine-producing region of Hungary, the great plain of the Danube which cuts the country in half southwards from Budapest, is the least known abroad. Its quantities of good ordinary wine, made from the country's most widely used grapes, Kadarka and Olasz Riesling, will probably find their way on to the thirsty world market before too long. Otherwise, the region around Lake Balaton in the south-west and the volcanic hills above Tokay in the north-east produce the best wines, together with the southern slopes of the Matra mountains halfway between Budapest and Tokay. In the last-named region Eger is the main town: its Bull's Blood is much liked in the U.K.

Hunter valley. The valley of the Hunter river in New South Wales, about a hundred miles north of Sydney, is the region where most of Australia's quality wines are made. Large producers like Lindeman and Penfold and smaller family concerns like McWilliam dominate production. Lindeman, who belong to the Phillip Morris empire, make Australia's biggest sellers here: the red Cawarra Claret from Shiraz and Grenache grapes, and white Ben Ean from a blend of Barossa Valley and Clare Valley wines.

hybrids. Grape vines developed through the cross-grafting of vinifera and labrusca (that is, European and American) vines.

I

imbottigliato. (I) Bottled.

imbottigliato dal produttore (all'origine), imbottigliato nell'origine. (I) Estate-bottled.

imbottigliato nella zona di produzione da . . . (I) Bottled on the estate of . . .

imbottigliato nello stabilimento della ditta . . . (I) Bottled in the cellars 'of the firm named', which does not have to be the producer.

Inferno. ◊ Valtellina.

infiascato. (I) Bottled in 'fiaschi', the straw-covered flasks used mainly in Tuscany.

infiascato alla fattoria. (I) Put into fiaschi at the winery.

Intreprinderile Agricole de Stat. Romanian state agricultural and wine-producing co-operative.

Isabel. Brand name for a range of Portuguese export wines which come as 'branco' (a Douro white with a good but rather sweet flavour), 'rosé' (very run-of-the-mill) and 'red' (a young Dão wine which can be drunk quite cool).

Ischia. ◊ Capri.

Israel. The culture of vines was revived here in the 1880s, but did not really expand until recently. Now the country's wine industry is growing rapidly and already has a sizeable share in the export market, especially to the United States. The hot dry summers do not make for quality wine, but modern mechanized processing allows at least decent table wines to be made. The reds, mostly from Grenache grapes, are better than the whites which use Muscat and Clairette but remain rather sweet whether still or sparkling. Virtually the only brand names known in the U.K. are Palwin and Camel. Their sweet red wines (of the kind mainly appreciated by park-bench winos) are numbered like Georgian ones. Camel's Elat white is dry and pleasant, but tastes like a Traminer grown in the wrong soil.

Italian wine laws. ◊ wine laws; for more specific information ◊ denominazione di origine controllata (both entries).

Italy. France and Italy have long disputed the various championships nations can win in the wine game. Italy now seems to hold all titles except the one for quality. It is the largest producer, with a larger acreage than France, and even the home consumption per head of the population is running neck and neck. The ever stricter application of the new laws (◊ wine laws) is meanwhile doing much to better Italy's export potential and to clear away the confusion which haphazard name-giving had created both at home and abroad. Perfectly well-known names like Orvieto, Brolio, Ruffino, Nebbiolo, Lacrima Christi and Garibaldi were hardly dictated by common criteria: they are the names of a place of origin, a castle which serves as a trade image, a producer, a grape, somebody's fancy, and a historical figure associated rather tenuously with the wine that bears his name. Although the more popular names will undoubtedly remain in use, the label will start to show more, and more pertinent, information as well. We will probably see an ever larger number of Italian wines on the U.K. market, where until now they have been much neglected. There are endless quantities of very good red and white table wines to be found, and cheap but drinkable dessert wines.

For more detailed introductions to the main wine-producing regions ◊ Alto Adige, Campania, Friuli, Lazio, Piedmont, Sardinia, Sicily, Tuscany and Veneto.

J

Japan. Has taken to wholesale production of whisky, but as yet does not produce wine in any quantity or, apparently, quality. American vine varieties are being planted, and more recently also Sémillon and Cabernet, mostly in Yamanashi province west of Tokyo. It seems likely that in the near future the quality will be improved and bulk shipment of table wines be started. So far, I have not seen any for sale in the U.K.

Jasnières. This small area on the Loir (itself a small tributary of the Loire) north of Tours makes a sweetish white wine like those of Vouvray.

Johannisberg. The vineyards of this Rheingau 'Bereich' between Geisenheim and Winkel are away from the Rhine, on the higher slopes dominated by Schloss Johannisberg which completely obscures the village itself. The commoner wines are still excellent, both in quality and value.

There is another Johannisberg, making quite passable white wine from Sylvaner grapes, in the Valais canton of Switzerland.

Jour de Fête. Brand name of Balls Brothers for a Beaujolais.

Juliénas. It is said that the Juliénas region grew vines before any other part of Beaujolais. The wine is darker and has more body than that of its next-door neighbour Saint-Amour, but it is as fresh and fruity. It does not seem to improve much beyond perhaps three or four years.

Jura. A tiny area of the Jura, from Lons-le-Saunier northward, makes a surprising variety of wines on slopes facing west towards Chalon. The most highly prized of its four ACs is Arbois, at the northern end. The white wines are dry and low in alcohol, most reds are soft and smooth. The best reds are made from a grape known locally as Plant d'Arbois: these are light enough in colour to be called 'pelure d'oignon'. The pink wines, known as vin gris, are in a class of their own.

Justina. Brand name of Gilbey Vintners (London) for their Portuguese wines, all shipped by Serra from the region just above Lisbon called Estremadura and more especially from its main red-wine district Ribatejo. Reputedly one of the ten best-selling wines in the U.K. (it is frequently seen in pubs) and of fair quality. The sweet white came out tops in the *Which?* guide. They all need drinking in one sitting, though. I have horrible memories of drinking the remainder of a bottle of the pink the next day – a clue to the reason why they often taste so foul in pubs.

K

Kabinett. (G) The lowest grade of Qualitätswein mit Prädikat.

Kadarka. The commonest red grape of Hungary and of the Balkan countries. It produces strong, full-bodied wines of which Bull's Blood is the best known. Most others are sold under the varietal name, with the addition of a region of origin, sometimes no more than the country. The blue grapes can produce very different wines on different soil, from an aromatic dark red to the pale pinks of the great plain of Hungary.

Kaiserstuhl. ⟡ Baden.

Kalebaǧ. ⟡ Turkey.

Kalterersee. ⟡ Alto Adige.

Kasel. The most important wine place on the Ruwer, its vineyards largely belonging to estates like the Bischöfliches Weingut in Trier. In good (hot) years Kasel makes some of the most fragrant wines of the whole Moselle-Saar-Ruwer region.

Kefraya. ⟡ Lebanon.

Kéknyelü. ⟡ Badacsony.

Kelibia. ⟡ Tunisia.

Kellerabzug. (G) Bottled in the proprietor's cellars.

Kellerei. (G) The cellars of a wine merchant.

Kellereiabzug. (G) Bottled by the merchant, not the producer.

Kellereigenossenschaft. (G) Wine-producers' co-operative.

KEO. Best known of the large Cyprus wine producers. Their wineries at Limassol produce dependable table wines, including one single-vineyard wine of quality called Domaine d'Aliera.

Kinloch, Charles. ⟡ Auberge; Bon Esprit.

Klevner. A variety of Traminer much used in Baden and northern Switzerland.

Kokkineli. Pink wine of Greece and Cyprus. The darkest and best ones come from the Peloponnese, more especially Nemea, south of Corinth.

Kolossi. One of the larger producers of fairly cheap Cyprus wines, reliable ordinaries which are better with regional food than on their own.

Korkbrand. (G) Producer's or bottler's mark burnt into the cork.

Kreuznach. More correctly Bad Kreuznach, but the first word seldom occurs on a wine label. A large spa on the Nahe, the centre of that region's wine production, with too many individual vineyards to even list here. Most of the cheaper wine is sold, through a large co-operative, simply as Kreuznacher.

Kriter. Reputedly the biggest-selling sparkling wine in France, available here in anything from quarter bottles to magnums.

Kröv. On the Moselle, downstream from Ürzig and therefore outside the best area, Kröv is known more for the seaside-postcard quality of its Nacktarsch label than for the quality of the wine itself.

Ksará. ⟡ Lebanon.

Kung Fu. ⟡ China.

K.W.V. Ko-operatieve Wijnbouwers Vereniging. A South African national co-operative, with five wineries and the country's biggest processing plant, which has become the semi-official overlord of the whole South African wine and spirits trade.

L

Lacrima Christi. At its best, a very pleasant and delicate white wine, quite dry despite a strong fragrance which hints of sweetness. It comes from a mixture of grapes on the seaward slopes of Vesuvius, and until the new wine laws begin to bite in that southern part of Italy as much indifferent rubbish will continue to be sold under this name as under Liebfraumilch.

Lago di Caldara. ⋄ Alto Adige.

Lalande de Pomerol. North of the Pomerol parish proper, Lalande and Néac produce reds which are only slightly less rounded but usually quite a bit cheaper than the increasingly popular Pomerol wines.

Lamarque (Château de). ⋄ Cussac.

Landwein. (G) Unclassified local plonk, the lowliest vin de pays.

Languedoc. Name of an ancient French province which took in the coastal region between the mouth of the Rhône and Narbonne. It includes part of the modern départements of Gard, Hérault and Aude – a bottomless reservoir of vin ordinaire. Some of the better wines are gaining a hold in the cheaper end of the export market, and names like Corbières, Fitou and Minervois are found on any U.K. merchant's and many a restaurant's lists.

late-bottled. Describes port of a lesser vintage which has been left to mature in wood before bottling.

Lauffen. ⋄ Württemberg.

laying-down. ⬦ storing.

Lazio. The hill country around Rome is, of course, one of the
oldest wine-producing regions of Italy, and the Castelli
Romani whites (especially Frascati) are justly famous. The
area around Lake Bolsena, north of Rome, borders on
Umbria and its wines (with the exception of Est est est)
have close connections with Orvieto with which they share
the same volcanic soil.

Lebanon. Modern viticulture in the Lebanon goes back to
1857, when a group of Jesuits founded what is still the
largest winery in the country at Ksará, on the road to
Damascus. Its vineyards, in the Beqa'a valley where the
Romans also cultivated vines, were not hit by phylloxera
until about 1915. They have since been replanted with
rather undistinguished French grapes producing better
red wines than white. Kefraya, Mansoura and Musar are
the main wine villages.

lees. Sediment formed on the bottom of the casks during
fermentation. Most wines are separated from their lees
fairly early, but a few acquire their special taste from being
bottled as they come (⬦ tiré sur lie).

Léognan. ⬦ Graves.

Liebfraumilch. Popular name for light, medium-sweet
blended wines made in the Rhine districts. The name
originated in Worms, at the southern edge of Rheinhessen,
with a vineyard belonging to the Liebfrauenkirche. The
cheaper varieties preserved their 'natural' sweetness with
massive doses of sulphur dioxide and now use other equally
unnatural means to the same end. Quality can vary greatly,
and prices vary just as much but often without reference to
quality. Even the big-selling brands like Blue Nun, pleasant
enough without being anything special, can be found at
very different prices.

light. Low in alcohol content, and usually mild in taste.

Limoux. The great speciality of Limoux, on the river Aude just above Carcassonne, is Blanquette de Limoux, a sweetish white sparkler with its own AC, made from a local grape, called Mauzac. The still wine is now also to be found in the U.K.

Lindeman. ♦ Hunter Valley.

Lion d'Or. Brand name of Nicolas for a slightly sweet white wine which tastes like Alsatian.

liquoroso. (I) Sweet, syrupy.

Lirac. Long known here only for producing a slightly lowlier relative of Tavel rosé, Lirac is now also gaining a reputation for red wines which for body and bouquet are among the best of the southern Côtes du Rhône.

Listrac. ♦ Moulis.

Livermore Valley. ♦ California.

Liversan, Château. ♦ Saint-Sauveur.

Loire. Although Loire wines are usually thought of as a close-knit family of elegant white wines, the differences between the various regions are considerable, and not nearly all the wines are white. The vineyards of Sancerre and Pouilly, farthest up the river, do indeed make very good dry whites, but those of the Orléans region are (no doubt rightly) made into vinegar. The Touraine wines are much sweeter, Anjou is best known for its pinks, and the Loire Atlantique produces large quantities of wholly indifferent wine called Gros-Plant du Pays Nantais and more rewarding Muscadets. For reds ♦ Bourgeuil, Chinon.

Loupiac. On the north bank of the Garonne, opposite the Barsac region, a few small communes make the better wines of the Premières Côtes de Bordeaux and therefore have the right to use their own name. Cadillac, Loupiac and Sainte-Croix-du-Mont all make sweet whites of the same strength as Sauternes and, at the cheap end of the market, considerably more palatable.

Lou Picassou. Brand name for three French-bottled wines from the hills around Aix-en-Provence. They are of VDQS standard, and as usual for the region the red is full-bodied and rather better than the white and pink, both of which are strictly for chilled summer drinking.

Ludon. ⟡ Macau.

Lussac–Saint-Émilion. ⟡ Saint-Georges–Saint-Émilion.

Lutomer Riesling. Unpretentious white wine named after the town of Ljutomer in the north-east of Yugoslavia, made from Italian Riesling varieties known locally as Laski Rizling and Renski Rizling. Its rise to probably the most sold dry white wine in the U.K. is the success-story of the late Richard Teltscher who single-handedly made this country aware of Yugoslav wines – and Yugoslavia aware of its foreign-market potential.

Luxembourg. Where the border with Germany is formed by the Moselle, Luxembourg is rapidly developing a substantial wine industry based on the Riesling grape and the Rivaner (as the Müller-Thurgau is called here). New legislation prevents the better wines from disappearing anonymously into German Sekt, but so far none of the local names of these very light and fragrant wines has become familiar in the U.K. They are worth looking out for and trying.

Lynch-Moussas, Château. ⟡ Saint-Sauveur.

M

Macau. Macau and, even higher up the river, Ludon are the beginning of the Haut-Médoc. Each can boast only one cru classé, but both have a largish number of cru bourgeois vineyards making solid drinking wine of exceptional quality but not yet of exceptional price.

Mackinlay-McPherson. ▷ Chiqua; Santiago.

Mâcon. A small provincial town on the Saône which does not produce any wine but gives its name to the Mâconnais, a large area between Chalonnais and Beaujolais. The wines of this area are pleasant and reliable, but on the whole so undistinguished that hardly any merit more than the simple A C Mâcon or Mâcon Supérieur (a difference in degree of alcohol merely). The ordinary whites made solely from the Chardonnay grape often go under the varietal name Pinot-Chardonnay, to distinguish them from the equally common but inferior Aligotés. The best whites have their own appellation, Mâcon-Villages.

Mâcon-Pissé. ▷ Pouilly-Fuissé.

Mâcon-Villages. This A C is given only to the better white wines of the Mâconnais. A few of the producing villages also have a right to use their own name; Pouilly-Fuissé is the only well-known one.

Madeira. Early colonists in the Far East, not allowed to import wines direct from Europe, used Madeira as their loophole. The island's wine was fortified to withstand the long voyage and fair boiled to death crossing the Equator: it lost a lot of its acidity and improved beyond belief. Now-adays, this process is simulated in 'estufas' (ovens). Four types of sweet wine are the result, distinguished by their grapes. In descending order of sweetness these are Malmsey, Bual, Verdelho and Sercial.

maderization. Oxidation, by which both the colour and the taste of a white or pink wine are darkened.

Madiran. One of the rarer French wines occasionally to be met in the U.K. Madiran itself is a small town at the very top of the Hautes-Pyrénées département, south of the Armagnac region of Nogaro. The wine is a strong red, aged in the cask for several years before being bottled.

maduro. (P) Mature.

magnum. Bottle holding twice the normal amount, that is approximately a litre and a half. The supermarket trade uses the word 'doubles' for this size, rather confusingly as there are more double-litres than double-bottles on the cheap market.

Magyar Állami Pincegazdaság. Hungarian state cellars.

Malaga. A sweet dark-brown fortified wine made in Anda-lusia from Pedro Ximenez and Muscat grapes by the solera method. Once popular as a dessert wine, it is now used mostly for cooking.

Malbec. This used to be one of the most important grapes of Bordeaux, but it is largely being abandoned because it tends to drop its fruit in the early stages. It is still used for the more common wines of south-western France and is the principal grape not only of Cahors but of most Argentinian red wines.

Malena. Brand name for a wide range of Yugoslav wines produced by the N.A.V.I.P. concern in Belgrade and distributed in the U.K. by French & Foreign Wines (London). They are all single-grape wines distinguished simply by varietal names. There are four whites, a pink and

malic acid

two reds (Prokupac and Cabernet). The latter two and also
the Riesling are unbelievably cheap if you can afford to
buy them a dozen litre-bottles at a time. Ideal party wines.

malic acid. The substance which gives unripe grapes their
sour taste.

Malmsey. English name of the Malvasia grape from which
the sweetest and darkest Madeira is made.

malolactic fermentation. After bottling the malic acid in
the wine can convert by a secondary fermentation into
lactic acid and carbon dioxide, so giving the slight sparkle
which is characteristic of wines like Vinho Verde. The process can be induced artificially.

Malvasia. Italian wines made from this grape (⟡ next entry)
are usually called by the varietal name followed by a place
of origin. The best of them are attractive golden dessert
wines, and the best of these come from the Aeolian islands
(Malvasia di Lipari) and from the Sicilian coast opposite
the islands (Malvasia di Milazzo). Sardinia makes similar
ones as does the Greek island of Rhodes. In Apulia the
grape also makes dry versions, and in Friuli in the far north
only light dry table wines.

Malvoisie. One of the oldest wine-producing grapes still
in active use. Its name is said to derive from Monemvasia
in the Peloponnese. It also goes under the Italian name
Malvasia and the old English form Malmsey. It is used all
around the Mediterranean, mostly for sweet wines.

Mañana, La. ⟡ Fine Fare.

Mansoura. ⟡ Lebanon.

Manzanilla. A very dry white wine produced west of Jerez,
around the river port Sanlúcar de Barrameda, from the
same grapes and by the same methods as sherry.

Margaux. The small town of Margaux, in the south of the
Haut-Médoc, is closely surrounded by a dozen crus
classés – the most astonishing cluster of great vineyards

anywhere in the world. None of their wines, nor any made in neighbouring Cantenac, comes anywhere near our price range – and the area doesn't have space for any 'undiscovered' cru bourgeois.

Maribor. ⟡ Yugoslavia.

Markgräferland. ⟡ Baden.

Marks & Spencer. Most branches which have food departments sell an ambitious and apparently still growing range of French and assorted other wines. They are usually of AC status, and they all bear labels which show both the exact measure of their contents and the alcohol percentage. The latter goes from 8 for the Moselle to $12\frac{1}{2}$ for the French reds: Beaujolais, Claret, Côtes du Rhône, Côtes de Provence and Côtes du Roussillon. There is also a Chianti and the cheapest red is the Spanish Vino Tinto. The whites include Mâcon-Villages, a Loire, Yugoslav Riesling, a Liebfraumilch, medium and really sweet Bordeaux. There was a cheap white Anjou, there now is an Anjou rosé as well. The most remarkable bargain in the list was its most expensive wine, a good sparkling white, probably Saumur.

Marques de Murrieta. One of the very best producers in the Rioja, not only for the traditional red wines of the region but also for its rarer dry whites.

Marques de Riscal. Another very dependable producer of quality wine in the Rioja.

Marquis de Saint-Estèphe. Brand name used by a co-operative of small growers in Saint-Estèphe for their 'ordinary' wine which lives up to all the exceptionally high standards of the parish.

Marsala. A rich sweet dessert wine, from the hot flat plains of western Sicily, which rivalled Madeira for Victorian popularity. It is fortified, partly with a sweet wine made from dried grapes, partly with unfermented must cooked to a syrup. The good ones are often blended on the solera system: these are never cheap. Most of the cheaper ones are rightly thought of as cooking wine.

Martillac. ⟡ Graves.

Mascara. Wines from the limestone hills in the south-east of Oran province, Algeria. The reds are smooth but heady, the pinks said to be full-bodied and fragrant, and the whites indifferent.

Masson, Paul. One of the great names in California wine-making. The original Paul Masson, from Burgundy, married the daughter of Charles Lefranc who ran the already famous Almadén vineyards. In the 1880s Masson established his own vineyards in the Santa Cruz mountains below San José. He ran them himself with increasing success until 1936. The new vineyards are farther south, near Soledad, but their wines, all known by varietal names, are still among the best of the region. Among those available in the U.K. the Pinot Noir is very good, the Zinfandel rather disappointing (good Zinfandels are rare anyway).

Mateus Rosé. A reasonably pleasant pink wine from Vila Real in the Douro region of Portugal. The promotion campaign, which established its current popularity, exploiting the then unusual shape of the bottle and a label which John Betjeman thought the prettiest of all, was perhaps more impressive than the wine. It can often be found at 'cut' prices, but cut from just what is hard to determine since there does not seem to be a recommended retail price.

Matrasa. ⟡ Azerbaijan.

Mavrodaphne. A very sweet red wine made from the grapes of the same name. The best varieties come from the northern part of the Peloponnese. It matures for several years in open vats before being bottled. The word Mavro, meaning black, is used as a prefix for a number of similar wines: the best of these are Mavro Romeiko from Crete and Mavroudi from Delphi.

Mavron, Mavrud. ⟡ Bulgaria, Cyprus.

Médoc. The greatest wine-producing area of Bordeaux, and therefore to many the best wine country in the world, runs along the left bank of the Gironde from the very end of the Garonne almost down to the sea. It is a narrow region of gravel banks washed up by the very wide and climate-tempering river, with a gradually increasing proportion of clay. From Saint-Estèphe to the sea this clay becomes sufficient to affect the drainage and thereby diminish the quality of the wine. Wine from this last region is simply called Médoc, while the region from Saint-Estèphe upstream is not only known as Haut-Médoc but also subdivides itself more jealously and more prolifically than any other wine region anywhere (⟡ cru classé).

Mendoza province. ⟡ Argentina.

Mercurey. A small area between Rully and Givry produces the best red wines (and some rare whites) of the Chalonnais region. They are rich and fruity, with a fine bouquet like the wines of Beaune, but show no particular inclination to improve with age.

Merlot. The most important black grape used for high-quality Bordeaux after the Cabernets with which it is usually blended. Merlot wines are softer, and the character of the blends varies with the proportion of Merlot to Cabernet. It also grows very well in northern Italy and northern Yugoslavia, and more recently in the Ticino region of Switzerland.

Metaxas. ⟡ Greece; Retsina.

méthode champenoise. The method of producing sparkling wine which is used in making Champagne. A second fermentation, the one which produces the carbon dioxide and with that the sparkle, is allowed to take place in the bottle, not in a cask as in the cheaper and less exacting cuve close method.

Meursault. The white wines of Meursault may have no grands crus like neighbouring Puligny-Montrachet, but their general standard is probably higher, and their distinctive (nutty?) taste happens to be my favourite. Only the minor ones still come within the monetary terms of this guide, but for those lucky enough to find some, the great ones of good years (Les Perrières 1969 or 1971) will live for something like fifteen years. For Meursault reds ⊳ Volnay.

mild. Of low acidity. Such wines should be drunk young, for they will not mature.

Minervois. This large area north of the Corbières hills forms part of the Languedoc and has produced wine since Roman days. Its warm dry climate makes excellent VDQS reds from the usual Grenache and Carignan grapes: well balanced, nicely fruity and of a lively colour, these are much better than the region's whites and pinks.

mis(e) en bouteilles. (F) Bottled, bottling.

mis(e) en bouteilles à la propriété, mis(e) en bouteilles au château, mis(e) en bouteilles au domaine. (F) Bottled at the place of origin.

mis(e) en bouteilles dans nos caves. (F) Bottled 'in our cellars', which may be those of a merchant or shipper.

mis(e) en bouteilles par le propriétaire. (F) Bottled by the grower.

Mittelhaardt. Sub-district of the Rheinpfalz which produces the best wines of the whole region, on sand and gravel soil, from Riesling grapes. Its centre is Bad Dürkheim.

Mittelrhein. At nearly the same latitude as the Isle of Wight and the English coastal vineyards, this is Europe's northernmost real wine-region. The east flank of the Rhine, between Bonn and Koblenz, uses mostly Riesling grapes to produce passable table wines of no great individual character.

Monbazillac. Once the most famous of the sweet white wines of the Bergerac area, but in its cheaper versions quite as indifferent as the rest of them.

Montagne–Saint-Émilion. ⇨ Saint-Georges–Saint-Émilion.

Monte Campo. Brand name for three colours of cheap Italian pasta plonk, sold in litres and double-litres.

Monthélie. Just north of Meursault and next-door to Volnay, this village produces good red wine which is still under-priced in relation to its more famous neighbours.

Montilla. Clear dry wine made south of Cordoba from the Pedro Ximenez grape and processed much like sherry. It develops the same flor and is aged by the solera method, but does not have to be fortified. The sale under its own name is a recent development; earlier it was used to make 'amontillado' sherry.

Montlouis. The wines from this village on the left bank of the Loire, between Tours and Amboise, are very similar to those of Vouvray and until the Second World War they were actually sold under that name.

Montmartre. Brand name for a series of French double-litre wines of indifferent origin and matching taste.

Montravel. On either side of the N136 which leads from Bergerac to Bordeaux, west of Port-Sainte-Foy, lie the Montravel and Côtes de Montravel vineyards. Their white wines are slightly sweetish and generally rather indifferent.

Mór. At Mór, some fifty miles west of Budapest, a native grape called Ezerjó produces a powerful white wine with an alcohol content up to 14 per cent and a rich, full fruit flavour.

Morgex. Morgex, on the Dora Baltea river in Italy, before it reaches Aosta, claims to have the highest vineyards in Europe 'at the foot of the Mont Blanc'. They produce a dry, very light white, with a faint herby taste which goes well with things like strong-tasting cold food.

Morgon. One of the heavier of the nine crus of Beaujolais, made in a large area around Villié-Morgon, north of Brouilly.

Moriles. A small town near Montilla, famous for its very fine Finos which are mostly drunk very young, served chilled, as an aperitif.

Morocco. Wine production in Morocco is small and of recent date. Most of it is concentrated either in the plains which stretch from Fez to Rabat, or in the coastal regions south of Rabat. The first of these regions is Sidi Larbi which makes red wines, and south of Casablanca is the Boulaouane area where very pale dry pink wines are known by their French name of (vin) Gris.

Moscato d'Asti. Cheaper and usually sweeter version of Asti Spumante.

Moselblümchen. Brand name for one of the less appealing very light Moselle blends. It is sold at a rather astonishing number of different prices.

Moselle. A very general description for a rather wide range of German wines, corresponding to the German Moselwein – wine from the Moselle region. With the increased emphasis on international wine law enforcement, the term has gone out of use. For most of the wines it was applied to see next entry.

Moselle-Saar-Ruwer. The river Saar comes from Alsace and flows through the German border country between Saarbrücken and Trier where it joins the Moselle going inland to feed the Rhine at Koblenz. The Ruwer is a smaller tributary of the Moselle, from the north side of the Schwarzwälder Hochwald which separates the Moselle valley from that of the Nahe. For quality, the great area is the Middle Moselle region of Piesport and Bernkastel.

The dominant grape here, the Riesling, is at its best on the weathered slate of the Moselle and thrives in its cool climate. The slate drains like a sieve on the steep slopes, but also reflects all the sun's heat back on to the grapes. The result is usually lively, fruity, sweet to the taste but with enough acidity for a longer life.

Moulin à Vent. The darkest and heaviest wine of the Beaujolais region, with an uncharacteristic tendency to improve in the bottle.

Moulis. The vineyards of this commune and those of neighbouring Listrac, away from the river banks, are rather different from those of the rest of the Haut-Médoc on account of their limestone soil. Their red wines are as strong in body and bouquet as their grander cousins, but because they were never classed above cru bourgeois supérieur they are still to be had at reasonable prices – even the splendidly named and truly 'exceptional' Château Chasse-Spleen.

Moussec. Brand name for an English-made sparkling wine, also sold in pubs in split sizes. The 'dry' is sweetish, and there is nothing medium about the 'medium sweet'.

mousseux. (F) Sparkling.

muffa nobile. ⬦ noble rot.

Mukuzani. ⬦ Georgia.

Müller-Thurgau. A white grape developed in 1872 by Professor Müller (from Thurgau in Switzerland) out of a cross between Riesling and (probably) Sylvaner. Its grapes ripen early, have a high yield and a mild muscat flavour. Its wines are drunk young, seldom beyond four or five years, because of their low acidity. Long used very successfully in the Rheinpfalz and Luxembourg (where it is called Rivaner), it has also become the most popular grape for English vineyards.

Murfatlar. A golden and lusciously sweet Muscat wine from the Black Sea coast of Romania.

Musar, Château. One of the few good Lebanese wines

available in the U.K., a strong-flavoured dry white with a hint of resin. Better with spicy (Middle Eastern) food than on its own. There is a dearer rosé under the same name.

Muscadet. Name of a grape which is also known as Melon de Bourgogne. Harvested early and fermented very slowly while remaining on its lees, the grape gives its name to a group of pale fragrant white wines from the Loire Atlantique, traditionally supposed to go well with shellfish. The best-known and most plentiful is Muscadet de Sèvre et Maine, an A C so wide as to allow a good deal of difference in quality. Generally, it is a wine for which I have never developed a taste (the very different variety 'tiré sur lie' excepted) but most others praise its 'robust character and delicate flavour'. Cyril Ray has found the ultimate phrase for it: 'Muscadet is "great" in the same way that bread or rice is "great" – it matters a great deal to a great number of people.'

Muscat. A grape family which can have many different hues but always has a distinctive musky fragrance. It grows all around the Mediterranean, and although a good deal of it is used for table grapes, it also makes a large number of fruity wines including the sparkling Asti Spumante and Clairette de Die. Often the fruit taste is preserved by halting the fermentation before it is complete. Many sweet dessert wines from southern France are known by the varietal name and an indication of place of origin.

must. Unfermented grape juice.

must-weight. The number of grammes by which a litre of must is heavier than a litre of distilled water: this determines the alcohol content the resulting wine will have. Must-weight is used under the 1971 German wine laws as a legal criterion for classing wine. It is determined by the Oechsle gauge, in France by the less detailed Baumé scale: ▷ their respective entries.

N

Nackenheim. Small village just north of Nierstein in Rheinhessen, with a few large and well-known vineyards making
pleasant, fragrant Riesling wines.

Nahe. The Nahe is a smaller river running parallel to the
Moselle, between the ridges of Schwarzwälder Hochwald
and Pfälzer Bergland. It joins the Rhine at Bingen. The
area is one of the more versatile of German wine-producing
regions: it has a great variety of soils, and consequently
the wine shows great differences of quality and character.
The most used grape is again the Riesling, and the best
wines come from the small region of sandstone hills on the
north bank between Schlossböckelheim and Kreuznach.

Napa Valley. A long stretch of vineyards along the Napa
river, north of San Francisco between Yountville and
Calistoga. Their wines are among the best in California.
Known by the usual varietal names these wines are further
distinguished by the names of the wineries which produce
them – from south to north: Mondavi, Inglenook, Beaulieu,
Louis Martini, Beringer, Charles Krug, Stony Hill, all
making quality wines. Beaulieu's wines are distributed in
the U.K. by Avery's of Bristol, but only the less interesting
ones are within our range. See also Christian Brothers.

Narbağ. ◊ Turkey.

natur(rein), Naturwein. (G) Wine made without the addition of sugar. The term is still used in Austria, but in
Germany it became illegal under the 1971 laws.

N.A.V.I.P. ⟡ Malena.

Néac. ⟡ Lalande de Pomerol.

Nebbiolo. One of the really noble grapes of Italy, responsible for some of the country's best red wines, as Barolo
and Gattinara. The more common light-red wines it makes
throughout Piedmont are given the simple varietal name.
There is an amabile version of these which is not sweet but
just pleasantly soft, and a sparkling one which can be good
when drunk chilled on a very hot day.

négociant. (F) A wine merchant.

Negru de Purkar. ⟡ U.S.S.R.

nero. (I) Black, that is: very dark red.

Neuchâtel. White wine made from Chasselas grapes grown
in the chalky soil of the Jura. Very light, often slightly fizzy
by being 'tiré sur lie', sometimes made sparkling by the
méthode champenoise.

Neusiedl. Austrian village at the northern end of the Neusiedler See in Burgenland. Produces the more run-of-the-mill
whites of the area.

Neuweier. ⟡ Baden.

New York wines. ⟡ U.S.A.

Nicolas. French producers of good and popular blended
wines, traditionally sold in litre bottles with a small plastic
cap. Grants of St James's manage to keep the whole
remarkably reliable group at the cheap end of the market.
There are two whites, Chassepré and Lion d'Or; two reds
called Canteval and Vieux Ceps; and a pink called Sciatino.
See their individual entries.

Niederhausen. A village on the Nahe, between Kreuznach
and Schlossböckelheim, which has a long string of vineyards facing south-west or south and producing some of
the best wines of the region.

Nierstein. The most famous name in Rheinhessen, a village
just downstream from Oppenheim with extensive and very

good vineyards using Riesling vines. The Einzellage names usually follow the designation Niersteiner, but the combination most often met with (Niersteiner Domthal) is spurious: it does not necessarily accommodate wine which has ever so much as seen the town. 'Gutes Domthal', on the other hand, is a collective name which all Nierstein vineyards can use.

noble grapes. The varieties of grape which have traditionally been responsible for the best wines of a region, and which under the present wine laws will be the only ones allowed if the wine is to qualify for AC or similar status.

noble rot. The effect of the fungus *Botrytis cinerea* which rots the grape skin and causes evaporation of the water content, thus shrivelling the grape and sending its sugar content soaring. Wine made from such grapes will be lusciously sweet, and expensive.

non-vintage. A blend of wines of different years.

nouveau. (F) 'New', said of wine drunk within a few months of the harvest. Beaujolais nouveau is the most famous example.

Nuits-St-Georges. A busy but singularly unattractive market town about halfway between Dijon and Beaune. Its neighbour to the south, Prémeaux, is the beginning of the Côte de Nuits. The best wines of the region all come from farther north, and the reds of Prémeaux and Nuits itself all go under the simple AC of Nuits–St-Georges. The better vineyards hyphenate their name after this. Their wines are strong and generous and usually age well.

Nuragus. A dry white wine from Sardinia, unpretentious to the point of tastelessness, named after the island's main native grape. Long sent to the mainland for blending, it is now exported direct as a table wine.

Oberhaardt. The southernmost sub-district of the Rhein-pfalz, producing aromatic and rather heavy table wines (both red and white) from a great variety of grapes, but not from the Riesling used in the rest of the district.

Oechsle gauge. An instrument for determining must-weight, and thereby the sugar content of a natural wine. This is the basis for wine classification under the 1971 German wine laws. 75° Oechsle means a specific gravity of 1·075. The actual sugar content in grammes per litre is about a quarter of the Oechsle number (on 75 this would be about 18 grammes, corresponding to the first step of the ◊ Baumé scale).

Olasz Riesling. Hungarian name for the Italian variety of the Riesling grape. It is the most commonly used white grape of the country and also throughout the Balkans. Much of its wine is known simply by the varietal name, occasionally with a place of origin.

Oloroso. Sherries made from Palomino and Pedro Ximenez grapes and kept sweet by halting the fermentation halfway with alcohol.

Oppenheim. Largest town of the Rheinhessen wine area, bordering on the more famous Nierstein and producing much the same Riesling wines: mellow, with a fine bouquet, and not quite dry.

Oran province. ◊ Algeria.

Originalabfüllung. (G) Estate-bottled. Abolished under the 1971 wine laws.

Original-Kellerabzug. (G) Bottled in the proprietors' cellars. No longer used (⋄ previous entry).

Orlando. ⋄ Barossa Valley.

Ortenau. ⋄ Baden.

Orvieto. The real Orvieto is an abboccato of great charm and character, in perfect harmony with its beautiful home town sticking up out of the Umbrian plain on a huge slab of volcanic rock riddled with caves. It is made from grapes (mostly Trebbiano) which are left to contract noble rot after the harvest, in open casks in the caves. The result is remarkably light and fragrant. A dry white wine is now made as well, but although good it has none of the abboccato's charm. Red Orvieto is soft and smooth – everything young Chianti is not, although both are made from Sangiovese grapes.

Östrich. Below Hallgarten on the Rhine. Its wines are of no special distinction, but no Rheingau wine is ever really bad.

Othello. A very drinkable dry red wine from Cyprus, named after Shakespeare's governor of the island. Malta also produces a cheap red wine under this name.

P

Palatinate. ▷ Rheinpfalz.

Palette. This small area of limestone soils near Aix-en-Provence makes good white wines from Clairette grapes, fresh but full reds and pinks from Grenache and others. It is one of only four Provençal A Cs.

Palomino. The sherry grape.

palus. (F) The fertile alluvial soil of the river valleys in the Bordeaux area. Its vines have a high yield but do not produce any distinguished wines and are not allowed to be used for the A C wines of the region.

Palwin. ▷ Israel.

Pampette. Brand name of J. T. Davies & Sons (Croydon) for a range of cheap French wines marketed in anything from half bottles to double-litres. The 'House Claret' and Rosé explain themselves, the Sweet is a white Bordeaux of Entre-deux-mers quality, the Rouge a 'Burgundy' most likely from those southern parts usually called the Mâconnais, and the Blanc is a medium-dry Loire (Atlantique, probably).

Panadés. The region around Villafranca del Panadés, west of Barcelona, is known mostly for well-made sparkling wines. The most widely distributed of these is Freixenet.

Papazkarasi. ▷ Doluca.

Parsac–Saint-Émilion. ▷ Saint-Georges–Saint-Émilion.

Passe-tout-grains. AC for red and a few pink Burgundy wines made from a mixture of one-third Pinot Noir and

two-thirds Gamay grapes. Never great but usually quite
drinkable, and cheap.

passito. (I) Grapes which have been half dried in the sun.
Also used for the sweet wines made from such grapes.

pasteurization. The process of heating bottled wine in hot
water or bulk wine in a system of steam-heated pipes to
about 60°C. This kills both the bacteria in the wine and
any chance of further improvement. It is never done to
wine of any quality.

Paternina, Federico. One of the more frequently met with,
and fortunately also more reliable, Spanish wine producers
with extensive interests in the Rioja.

Pauillac. A sizeable small town on the Gironde, in the middle
of a long, narrow stretch of very grand Haut-Médoc vineyards. This is the classic Bordeaux region, including eigh-
teen of the sixty-two classed growths, three of them among
the five premiers crus. Even the lesser wines are well above
average, and some of the crus bourgeois can still be had at
surprising prices – even La Couronne, which is the only
cru exceptionnel. The large co-operative of smaller growers
uses La Rose-Pauillac as a brand name.

Pearl. A term which is gaining currency in Australia for
sparkling wine, whatever its production method and whatever its colour.

Pécharmant. ⟡ Bergerac.

Pech Vermeil, Château. ⟡ Corbières.

Pedro Ximenez. The outstanding white grape of Montilla,
Malaga and sweet sherries is said to derive from the
Elbling of Germany, brought to Spain by one Peter
Siemens. It seems to inspire such legends everywhere, for
in Argentina, where it is the main white grape, it is thought
to be native.

Peñaflor. ⟡ Argentina.

Penfold. One of the largest Australian wine-producing firms,

with vineyards and wineries in Barossa Valley, Coonawarra
and Hunter Valley. They make almost any type of wine,
including some sweet whites which are cheap even in the
U.K.

percentage. The alcohol percentage expressed on wine
labels is based on the continental or Gay-Lussac scale,
which indicates the exact volume percentage of absolute
alcohol in a liquid, determined at a standard temperature.
American percentages are double the Gay-Lussac figures.
The degrees of the Sykes scale are not percentages at all.

Perlaire. Brand name of Woolley Duval & Beaufoys for
Kingston-upon-Thames bottled French red, pink and
medium-dry white wines claiming no great standards and
rightly so.

perlant. (F) The quality of slight effervescence often found
in wine 'tiré sur lie'.

Perle d'Alsace. Of the sparkling wines of Alsace, this one
made by Dopff is one of the best as well as the cheapest.

Perlwein. (G) Wine which is very slightly sparkling, not
enough to produce a froth.

Pernand-Vergelesses. ⟡ Côte de Beaune-Villages.

pétillant. (F) Half-sparkling.

Petits Châteaux. Brand name for half a dozen very cheap
A C wines marketed by French Wine Farmers Ltd (London)
through shops like the Co-op. The range consists of a red
and a dry white Bordeaux, red Burgundy (described as
'rich and smooth'), Beaujolais and Côtes du Rhône, and
Anjou Rosé. The ones I tried were rather more than fair
value for their price.

Pez; Phélan-Ségur, Château. ⟡ Saint-Estèphe.

phylloxera. The *Phylloxera vastatrix* or vine louse is a small
beetle which lives off the roots of the vine. In the 1860s and
1870s it devastated virtually the whole of Europe's vineyards. It was first identified at Kew in 1863, and started its

way through France in Provence in 1865, reaching the Médoc by 1878 and Champagne by the 1890s. American vines (*Vitis labrusca*) had developed the ability to heal the wounds inflicted on the root, and it was found possible to graft the European *Vitis vinifera* plants on to the American roots, thus continuing the traditional sorts with a built-in immunity to the plague.

Piedmont. An enormous and varied region, stretching from the Alps through the Po valley to the coastal hills of Liguria. Turin, the vermouth centre, is its capital; Asti and the Val d'Aosta its main wine-producing regions. The main grapes are the Muscat (used to make sparkling wines only) and the marvellous Nebbiolo which makes some of Italy's best red wines.

Piesport. A Middle Moselle village in the midst of more than two miles of sloping vineyards which face due south and which are now collectively labelled under the name of the famous Goldtröpfchen. Across the river, in a much inferior situation, are the Gunterslay and Treppchen vineyards whose wines are more like those of neighbouring Dhron.

Pilton Manor. This 'vineyard replanted, originally established by the abbots of Glastonbury c1240' (as it says on its labels) lies on the side of the village of Pilton, near Shepton Mallet in Somerset. It uses mostly Müller-Thurgau grapes (labelling their wine as Riesling-Sylvaner) to produce a wine which is Alsatian in character rather than German. The newer Seyve-Villard produces an almost colourless much drier white wine which I like better. Both are good picnic wines, not much more. Buy them from the Wine Society, not from the vineyard where you pay about 20 per cent more (the view is good but can be had free).

Pineau de la Loire. This grape, also known as Chenin Blanc, makes the best wines of the middle Loire but does not seem to produce any notable wine outside that region.

Harvested late, it is often affected by noble rot but retains a high level of acidity which makes its wines age rather well. It should not be confused with the Pinot family, even if in California it is often called White Pinot.

Pinot Blanc. ⟡ Chardonnay.

Pinot Gris. Also called Tokay d'Alsace, this member of the Pinot family is reputed to be a variety which Lazarus von Schwendi brought from Hungary after his famous siege of Tokay in the middle of the sixteenth century. In Baden it is known as Ruländer. In most areas its use is declining owing to its poor yield, but its white wines are full, smooth and good tasting. Northern Italy, on the other hand, is experimenting quite successfully with the Pinot Grigio.

Pinot Noir. The small, tightly bunched black grape which produces the finest wines of Burgundy and Champagne, but is rarely as good when used elsewhere. Its German version, the Spätburgunder, makes soft light-coloured wines. In Alsace its pink wines have the varietal name as their A C.

Pinson, Le. Brand name for medium-overpriced dry white and light red French table wines, bottled in litres by Finch.

plonk. The origin of this popular word for cheap wine has not been established with any certainty, but the most likely source seems to be vin blanc as mispronounced by soldiers in the First World War. The oldest known use in print is in H. Williamson's *Patriot's Progress* (4:137). Examples of Second World War use are mostly Australian. 'Everyday plonk' even appeared in *The Times* (25 August 1973, page 13).

Plonque. Brand name of Balls Brothers for four wines which their catalogue claims to be 'Appellation Controlee wines from top quality producers'. The labels say 'vin de pays', and that is what they taste like: honest, but no more than that. The dry and medium-sweet whites are Bordeaux, the pink comes from the Loire, and the red, long unspecified and at one time North African, is now a Côtes du Rhône.

Pomerol. A very small but quite distinctive area north-west of Libourne, where the river l'Isle joins the Dordogne. A gravel plateau, no more than about fifteen square kilometres, produces fine red wines which are softer and quicker to mature than most other Bordeaux. Their grape is the Merlot, not the Cabernet, and their character can be very near that of a good Burgundy. The number of individual vineyards using their own name is confusingly high, but no higher than the standards of the region: there simply is no such thing as an indifferent Pomerol. The great ones are as expensive as the best Médoc, but lesser growths like Clos l'Église and Clos René are still exceptionally good value for money.

Pommard. Between Beaune and Volnay, the vineyards of Pommard make one of the lighter of the great red Burgundies. They tend to be overpriced, but can still be found at auction.

Port. One of the most unusual wines in the world, if only for its production methods. The grapes grow in Portugal's upper Douro region on slopes so steep that no animal or mechanized transport is possible. They were long trodden by human foot, to extract the maximum in colourants and tannin: fermentation will be stopped very short by the addition of about one-third the volume in neat brandy. The wine is then sent down the river to Vila Nova de Gaia, opposite the harbour of Oporto (which gave the wine its name). Here it is kept in warehouses called lodges. In exceptionally good years a vintage is declared and the wine is bottled young and unblended. The bulk of the wine, however, is kept in wooden vats where it matures much faster: the standard blends are around five years of age.

White port is made of white grapes. It is not as sweet as the dark variety, and makes an excellent chilled apéritif.

Portugal. From Lisbon northwards the entire coastal region and a good deal of the middle mountains produce wine of a very high general standard, if often of no great individual distinction. The coast has an ideal climate, long warm summers followed by ample rain, and even the inland regions do not yet have the fierce land-climate of central Spain.

There are seven controlled regions (região demarcada) of AC standard. Four of these are around Lisbon and relatively small: Bucelas and Carcavelos produce mostly white wines, Colares reds, and Setúbal is famous only for its Moscatel dessert wines. Farther north are the uncontrolled regions of Estremadura, Ribatejo and Barraida, followed by the three huge demarcated areas of Dão, Douro and Vinho Verde. From the upper Douro comes the country's best-seller, port.

Few of the table wines are sold under specific regional names because it is customary to blend wines even from different regions. The brand names are those of bottlers and shippers, sometimes of U.K. distributors. Standards, especially for the cheaper varieties, are higher than for the corresponding bulk wines from Spain.

Portugieser. This early-ripening and high-yielding grape has become the most used black vine in Germany. Its wines, which have a delicate bouquet, are best drunk young: their low acidity will not allow them to improve with age. The Weissherbsts made from this grape are, to my taste, Germany's best pink wines.

Portvein. ⟡ Azerbaijan.

Pouilly-Fuissé. The twin villages of Pouilly and Fuissé command the stretch of limestone hills between the Mâconnais and Beaujolais where the Chardonnay produces

the best white Mâcon wines, dry and crisp but generous in
their distinctive greenish-yellow colour and their equally
distinctive smell. Pouilly-Loché and Pouilly Vinzelles come
from the southern end of the area, Mâcon-Pissé from the
north: they are all very similar.

Pouilly Fumé. One of the best white wines of the Loire.
Made from Sauvignon grapes (known locally as Blanc
Fumé) the wine is fragrant and dry, with a colour that
tends to green and a distinctive smoky taste.

Pouilly-sur-Loire. This name is restricted to the village's
delicate white wines made from Chasselas grapes. They
are low both in acidity and alcohol content and consequently do not develop at all. The area's Sauvignon wine
is called Pouilly Fumé (⊳ preceding entry).

Poujeaux. For château names beginning or ending with this
place-name ⊳ Moulis.

pourriture noble. ⊳ noble rot.

Prädikatswein. ⊳ Qualitätswein mit Prädikat.

Prémeaux. ⊳ Nuits-St-Georges.

premier cru. (F) Second rank of classed wines (preceded by
grand cru) in Burgundy; highest rating for Bordeaux wines.

Premières Côtes de Bordeaux. The right bank of the
Garonne, opposite the Graves region, is the only southern
part of Bordeaux to make as much red wine as white.
About forty villages here make red wines that are in fact
better than their sweetish white ones – an exception is the
extreme south of the region, around Loupiac.

price. With the cheaper wines, it is important to realize that
there is an unvarying amount (not a percentage) involved in
the price of a bottle of wine, which in no way reflects the
value or quality of what you buy. This amount represents
the cost of bottling and shipping (at least 15p each) and the
duty levied by H.M. Customs & Excise. At present the
duty alone on still table wine works out at more than 50p

a bottle – plus 8 per cent VAT. This means, very roughly, that for a bottle of wine which at 25p would show a fair profit for all concerned in its production, you have to pay a pound. Yet for £1.50 you would buy a wine which in itself could be nearly three times as expensive. Part of the economics of the increasingly popular doubles and double-litres is that the amount for the bottle and its transport is only marginally higher than that spent on a standard bottle with half or one-third the same contents.

Priorato. ◊ Catalonia.

Prokupac. Robust and fruity red wines from Serbia and Macedonia, named after a native grape. They are the vin ordinaire of the whole of south-eastern Yugoslavia. Some are very attractive, especially those made along the Morava river, some are so dark as to be almost bitter. The export variety, alas, is changing to a soft Rhône-like beverage. There is also a rosé from the same grape.

proof. The standard strength of all distilled alcoholic liquors, including wine and vinegar. By an Act of Parliament of 1820, known as 58 Geo. III, c. 28, this standard is 'a liquid which at 51°F weighs exactly twelve-thirteenths of the weight of an equal volume of distilled water'. These days the weight is taken at 60°F and the standard works out to be a mixture of water and alcohol containing 0·4924 absolute alcohol by weight or 0·5706 by volume. Liquors are tested by means of Sykes' hydrometer (◊ Sykes scale) which was legalized even earlier (56 Geo. III, c. 40). Compared with the standard a liquor is said to be so many per cent proof, or so many per cent under proof. The whole crazy practice seems to stem from gunnery: if gunpowder is moistened with a spirit which is 'under proof' it will not light.

The American proof system is based on a 50–50 mixture of water and alcohol. Most civilized countries express alcohol content in volume percentages, and it is at last a legal requirement even in the U.K. to show this percentage on all wine labels.

proprietary names. ⋄ brand names.

Prošek. A rather sweet, darkly golden wine made along the Dalmatian coast of Yugoslavia, from grapes which are dried in the sun before pressing.

Provence. The south-eastern part of France, roughly everything south of a line between Avignon and Nice. It comprises the administrative départements Bouches-du-Rhône and Var. Its wines are seldom above reasonable VDQS standards – those that are come from Bandol, Cassis or Palette. The pinks are better and better-known than the other ordinaries. Further notes under Côte de Provence and Coteaux d'Aix.

Puisseguin–Saint-Émilion. ⋄ Saint-Georges–Saint-Émilion.

Puligny-Montrachet. A village on the Côte de Beaune which is as famous for its white wines as Meursault, its neighbour a few miles to the north-east. The quality varies uncomfortably, but the best ones have no equals in Burgundy.

puttonyok. (H) Plural of puttonos. ⋄ Aszu.

Q

Q.b.A., Qualitätswein bestimmter Anbaugebiete. (G)
Wine which, by law, must be from a specified region
(Gebiet) and from specified grape varieties. It must also
attain a must-weight of 65 Oechsle, equivalent to $8\frac{1}{2}$ per
cent natural alcohol.

Qualitätswein mit Prädikat. (G) Applies only to quality
wines made without the addition of sugar. The wine must
be from a specified district (Bereich) and from specified
grapes. Beyond that, the 'Prädikat' (qualification) given
to any specific wine depends mostly on its must-weight.
Kabinett is the lowest class in this system, with a must-
weight of 75. Spätlese ('late gathering') follows with a
must-weight of 80. Auslese ('selective gathering' of ripe
grapes only) needs 90. In some cases grapes are left on the
vine until frost sends the sugar content up even higher;
then there are Beerenauslese (must-weight 120) and
Trockenbeerenauslese (150), and eventually Eiswein –
dessert wines of distinction, but of a price well beyond our
range.

Quarts de Chaume. ⟡ Coteaux du Layon.

Quincy. The white wines of Quincy and neighbouring
Reuilly are officially Loire ACs, but their region of origin
is on the Cher, near Bourges. They are dry but fruity,
made from Sauvignon grapes, and in character very like
their nearest Loire neighbour, Sancerre.

quinta. (P) Estate.

R

racking. The process of drawing off the fermenting wine from its lees.

rancio. Rancid, a Spanish word lovingly used in southern France for wine which has become maderized.

Ravello. Pleasant table wines (white, red, and a rather sweet pink) from the southern slopes of the Sorrentine peninsula, south of Naples. Among the best are those labelled Gran Caruso: the name refers to its producers, not to Enrico.

récolte. (F) Vintage.

red wine. Wine made from dark-skinned grapes which are de-stalked and broken, put into vats and left to ferment for five or more days before the newly made wine is run off the debris. Usually all the natural sugar of the must is converted into alcohol: sweet red wine, unlike sweet white, is usually fortified.

região demarcada. (P) Specific region, defined by law. There are seven of these in Portugal: see that country's main entry.

reinsortig. (G) Made of only one specified grape variety.

Rendez Vous. Brand name for French AC wines marketed, rather dubiously, at a uniform price: Bordeaux, Beaujolais and Côtes du Rhône. Honest enough, but decidedly from the thin end of very wide appellations and therefore with less character than many a good VDQS.

réserve. (F) A word which suggests it should mean something special, but doesn't. Anything can be 'kept back', for any reason.

Réserve Moutier. Brand name for a red Beaune and a white Mâcon shipped in bulk and bottled in London.

residual sugar. Sugar which remains in the wine when fermentation stops or is halted.

Retsina. The most famous wine of Greece, a very dry white of low alcohol content which is flavoured with resin (originally added as a conserving agent). It is a name which can be applied to many varieties, regardless of their place of origin. Consequently, the producer's or shipper's is the crucial name to look for. My own taste is for Metaxas, which is quite genteel. The rougher ones are lovely, too, but strictly for drinking with the food of the eastern Mediterranean.

Reuilly. ◇ Quincy.

Reynal. Brand name for pink and white Spanish table wines shipped by Pinord of Villafranca del Panadés and sold in fluted bottles with presumably English-printed labels which misspell the place name but give all relevant directions in Spanish. Since one of the wines is a slightly sweet slightly sparkling white which should be stored upright, this is perhaps not the best practice. The wines themselves are quite good value for their very low price.

Rheingau. Between Mainz and Bingen the Rhine flows east to west for some twenty miles, at the bottom of the foothills of the Taunus mountains. The slate soil, sloping south-wards to the river, produces polished wines of great character, with a deeper but less fruity flavour than the Moselles – although here, too, the Riesling is the main grape. The most widely known villages in the area are neighbouring Rüdesheim, Geisenheim and Johannisberg.

Rheinhessen. South of the Rheingau and east of the Nahe district, this area of many small rivers is divided into an even greater number of small vineyards with different soils growing different grapes and in consequence producing

some of the most individual wines in Germany. The best
ones come from Oppenheim and Nierstein and are Riesling-
based. The Sylvaner grape mostly makes a light and rather
dull wine marketed as Liebfraumilch whatever part of
the region it comes from.

Rheinpfalz. Known in England as the Palatinate, this largest
German wine region continues Alsace to the north in the
same way as its mountain range, the Haardt, continues the
Vosges mountains. The Rhine is the region's eastern border.
The main vineyards follow what is known as the Deutsche
Weinstrasse, where the slopes of the Pfälzer Wald gradually turn into the flat, wide and fertile lands of the river
valley. In wine-producing terms the long Weinstrasse is
divided into three sections (Ober-, Mittel- and Unterhaardt) which will be found discussed separately.

Rheinriesling. Name given in Austria to what is there considered to be the 'real' Riesling as distinguished from a
lowlier Italian variety which is also widely used. Despite
its name the Rheinriesling is sometimes said to be different
from the grape used so widely in Germany.

Ribatejo. Although it is not one of Portugal's regiãos demarcadas, this area along the Tejo (Tagus) river north of
Lisbon is one of the country's largest wine producers.
None of its red and whites is sold under regional names:
it all goes into the branded blends (Dom Bazilio, Castelo
Real, Justina) which form the greater part of Portugal's
table wine exports.

Ricasoli. ⟡ Chianti.

Richards, Château les. ⟡ Côtes de Bourg.

Ried. (G) Used in Austria to denote a vineyard. Similar to
the French clos.

Riesling. One of the best wine-producing grapes in the
world, a late-ripening white with small, closely packed
berries of a greenish-yellow tint. It is used for most of the

Moselle and all the better Rhine wines, and is rated the first of the cépages nobles in Alsace. The quality of its wines depends largely on the soil it grows in, but the end result is usually dry, crisp and aromatic. Of its many varieties, the Rheinriesling is used in Austria and Johannisberg Riesling in California, while the Italian version is famous throughout eastern Europe as Olasz Riesling.

Rioja. The only wine district in Spain which is at all well known for table wines of more than ordinary quality. Most of its wines are red, and their main grape is the Granacha – better known as the Grenache. These wines are still aged in vats for several years before bottling, which gives them a characteristic oak flavour. This practice is just one of many reminders that the area's viticulture was founded by Bordeaux growers who found (temporary) refuge from the phylloxera of their native vineyards.

The Rioja area follows the river Ebro for about a hundred kilometres, from Alfaro to the wine trade centre Haro. Up to Logroño it is the Rioja Baja, dry and hot, making heady wines mostly used for blending. North of Logroño lies the quality area, the Rioja Alavesa, where producers like the Marques de Riscal make some of the best red wine outside France. The Rioja Alta shares Alava's cooler and wetter climate and also makes fine wines which age well.

Riquewihr. This village about five miles north-west of Colmar is one of the few places in Alsace which consistently uses its own name rather than just one of the usual varietal names. Unfortunately this does not mean that its wines are also out of the ordinary.

riserva. (I) Unlike the French réserve, this term is indeed applied to wines of a better than average quality, originally 'reserved' for the proprietor but now subjected to legal requirements.

Rivaner. ⇨ Müller-Thurgau.

Romanello. Brand name for a light red and a very thin white wine from Lazio, bottled by Vinades of Frascati. ◊ Castelli Romani.

Romania. Although Romania is now something like the sixth or seventh largest wine-producer in the world, little of its product is seen in the U.K. Most of it comes from the southern half of the country, below the Carpathian mountains, and all of the good wines seem to be white. They are known by their grape variety, and the place of origin seldom gets any prominence. The main grapes are the inevitable Riesling (here, as in Yugoslavia, it is the Italian variety known as Olasz Riesling) and the native Feteascǎ, followed by the Hungarian Furmint. A small but interesting selection of Romanian wines is sold in the U.K. under the Astra brand label.

rosado; rosato. (S and P; I) Pink.

rosé. Pink wine. Such wines are usually made from crushed black grapes which spend only a very short time (a matter of hours) together with their skins, and finish their fermentation after separation from the debris. They must be bottled early and drunk within a couple of years, for none of them ages at all. Similar wines made from dark-juiced grapes separated immediately from their stalks and skins are known as vin gris and Weissherbst. Pink wines made from a mixture of red and white grapes include Rotling or Schillerwein as well as pink Champagne.

Rosé d'Anjou. ◊ Anjou.

Rosé de la Loire. One of the most recent ACs, reserved for dry pink wines.

Rose-Pauillac, (Château) la. Brand name used by the co-operative of small Pauillac growers for their 'ordinary' wine which may be somewhat lighter than its classed cousins but is still hardly ordinary by most wine-drinkers' standards.

Rossellino. Brand name for three colours of wine the Italians must have been glad to see go.

rosso; rosu. (I; R) Red.

Rotling. German name for pink wine made from a mixture of red and white grapes. The better ones are usually labelled Schillerwein.

Rotwein. (G) Red wine.

rouge (F). Red.

rough. Descriptive term for wine in which tartaric acid dominates the taste.

Rousselle, Château. ⟡ Côtes de Bourg.

Roussillon. In official wine classification this area, roughly the same as the Pyrénées Orientales département, gets lumped together with the Languedoc which is less easy to define geographically. The speciality of Roussillon lies in fortified wines (vins doux naturels) which are sweet dessert whites carrying a higher classification than the area's red wines. The reds of the northern section are grouped with those of the Corbières hills, those of the middle use the AC name Côtes du Roussillon. In the far south, near the Spanish border, the Banyuls region has its own AC. Otherwise, much Roussillon wine is VDQS without too much emphasis on the place of individual origin.

ruby. Descriptive term for port aged in the wood for a few years only and still retaining its dark colour and full flavour.

Rüdesheim. The best vineyards of this Rheingau village are straight opposite the mouth of the Nahe at Bingen: all their wines are distinguished by having the word Berg before the name of the individual vineyard. But even the wines of lesser sites, away from the river on gentler slopes, are among the best of the whole region.

Ruiz Belmonte. ⟡ Franchette.

Ruländer. A white grape belonging to the Pinot family

(▷ Pinot Gris). It requires a very good soil. Its small, tight, greyish-red grapes make remarkably heavy wines. They are used to good effect in several parts of Germany, in northern Italy and in the Balkans where their name is sometimes bastardized to Rulanda.

Rully. Dry, fruity, golden wine made in the Chalonnais from Chardonnay grapes. Although not much liked in France, the wine is rapidly going up in price. So far, it has remained quite accessible at auction. Red Rully is very similar to Mercurey, its nearest neighbour to the south.

Ružica. Serbo-Croat for pink, and hence the 'name' under which this type of fresh Yugoslav wine is sold in the U.K.

S

Sables–Saint-Émilion. A very small wine region on the right bank of the Dordogne, south of Libourne. No great names here, but good wines at lower prices than usually paid for Saint-Émilion. The AC ceased to exist at the end of 1973.

sack. Although probably a bastard form of sec, this is the oldest English term for sweet wines like sherry, Malaga and Madeira.

Safeway. The Safeway supermarkets sell three colours of French wine under their brand label, as well as a 'Spanish full-bodied red'. All are quite cheap, but no better than one might expect.

Sainsbury. Their dismal range of Spanish plonk included a 'Burgundy', medium dry and even sweeter whites, and something pink. Under its new name Vino de Catalonia its packaging has undergone a considerable face-lift without any beneficial effects on its quality. The firm's 'Moroccan red', from Grenache grapes, looks like beetroot juice but remains remarkably honest for its rock-bottom price: you can even finish a bottle the next day without coming to active harm.

Saint-Amour. The lightest of the wines of Beaujolais, both in colour and in body, from the far northern end of the region.

Saint-Aubin. West of Chassagne-Montrachet, at the southern edge of the Côte de Beaune. No famous or even separately named crus here, just good dependable wine, both red and white.

Saint-Chinian. The wines of the upper reaches of the river Orb, an area which borders in the south-west on the Minervois, now have this name as their own VDQS. Previously, Saint-Chinian was one of the best communes using the Coteaux du Languedoc label.

Saint-Christol, Saint-Drézéry. ◊ Coteaux du Languedoc.

Sainte-Croix-du-Mont. ◊ Loupiac.

Saint-Émilion. A large area, lying east of Libourne and northwards from the banks of the Dordogne, uses Saint-Émilion as its generic appellation. The 'real' Saint-Émilion district is much smaller. It continues the plateau of Pomerol eastwards and centres on the twin hills of Saint-Émilion itself and of Château Troplong-Mondot. The character of the wines here is close to Pomerol, too: the same soil, the same Merlot grapes, the same confusion of small vineyards. On the border with Pomerol it is the Figeac group which dominates the scene: Châteaux Figeac, La Tour Figeac and La Tour du Pin Figeac all make very fine wine. On the slopes south of Saint-Émilion châteaux like La Clotte and Grandes-Murailles are still good value against the high prices of more famous neighbours.

The surroundings of this small area have more clay and lime in their soil and their wine is nearer 'ordinary' clarets than are those of the Pomerol and Saint-Émilion parishes. Five of the more important villages use their own names hyphenated before the general appellation: Saint-Georges, Lussac, Montagne, Parsac and Puisseguin.

Saint-Estèphe. Of the four great communes of the Haut-Médoc this one is nearest to the sea, and already the gravel banks of the river begin to show more and more clay. The result is higher acidity but also a higher tannin content: the wines here are very deep in colour, firm and full, reliable and with excellent ageing ability. The district has few crus classés, but the largest number of crus bourgeois supérieurs, and no 'bad' wines at all. Phélan-Ségur and Canteloup, next door to each other and to Saint-Estèphe itself, are still excellent value for money – so are Château Beau-Site at Saint Corbian and the two small châteaux of Pez. A large growers' co-operative uses the name Marquis de Saint-Estèphe.

Saint-Georges. ♦ Coteaux du Languedoc.

Saint-Georges–Saint-Émilion. The twin villages of Saint-Georges and Montagne, just north of Saint-Émilion itself, as well as the larger Lussac to the north-east, Puisseguin to the east and Parsac to the south-east of them, have a right to use their own names hyphenated before the regional appellation. The number of individually named vineyards here is very large, but standards are high and most of the wine is very good indeed. Even that of Château St-Georges itself can still be found within our price range.

Saint-Joseph. General name for quite good red wines from a long stretch of vineyards along the right bank of the Rhône valley between the Côte Rôtie and Tournon.

Saint-Julien. Within the limitations of this guide, the small parish of Saint-Julien is probably the least interesting part of the whole Médoc. Just upstream from Pauillac and dominated by the huge Léoville group of estates, it produces little wine that is not classed, and the little that is not should be and is already priced accordingly.

Saint-Laurent. ♦ Cussac.

Saint Panteleïmon. A very sweet white wine from Cyprus.

Saint-Pourçain. North of the Massif Central, between the Sioule and the Allier rivers, a crisp and very dry white wine is made which merits more than its present VDQS status and which consequently is very good value for money (where it can be found at all).

Saint-Sauveur. Small parish inland from Pauillac which includes one classed growth, Château Lynch-Moussas – not nearly as well known as Lynch-Bages and therefore considerably cheaper, especially at auction – and some reliable lesser vineyards like Château Liversan.

Saint-Seurin-de-Cadourne. The seaward edge of the Haut-Médoc does not yet reach the high standards of neighbouring Saint-Estèphe but makes excellent wine which already ages better than its lowland Médoc neighbours and which at the moment is among the best value-for-money buys of all Bordeaux. Châteaux like Coufran and Verdignan, although farthest out to the sea, make the most reliable wines, well worth looking for.

Saint-Vérand. Wine from the Pouilly-Fuissé area, indistinguishable from its more famous cousins but so far considerably cheaper.

Salinas Valley. ⟡ California.

Salvo. Brand name of Capital Wine & Travers (London) for a series of double-litre wines from Piedmont. The white, curiously, is labelled Riesling: this grape has never done well in the region, and its wines have never been thought much of there. There seems little reason to think any better of them here.

Samos. A sweet, golden wine from the island of Samos in the Dodecanese, the archipelago close to the Turkish coast south of Izmir. The cheaper versions, although not as sweet, are a good deal more cloying.

Sancerre. Although the main grape is always the Sauvignon, there is a great deal of difference between the dry white wines from individual vineyards surrounding this small sleepy hill town on the Loire. Apart from position the main reason for these differences is the soil, which is usually chalky but with patches of flinty ground in between. Wines from the latter have character very early, but do not improve it; the others age to beautiful firm and fragrant wines.

San Fernando. Brand name for 'estate bottled' Spanish wines shipped from Tarragona. The dry white tastes like an indifferent Alella – the Menorquin version of which I find especially sickly. Odd there should be no Priorato red in this low-priced range.

San Gimignano. ◊ Vernaccia.

Sangiovese. Name of the grape from which Chianti is made, and the varietal name of the full-bodied red wines it makes in other parts of Italy, notably throughout Emilia-Romagna but increasingly also on Sardinia.

Sans Chichi. Brand name of Wine Agencies London for red and white French wines. At the moment the red is fruity and the white quite dry, but their region of origin varies from time to time. The white seems to come mostly from south-west Bordeaux and the Dordogne.

Sansovino. Brand name for Italian ordinaries marketed in the U.K. by Grants of St James's. They are quite good, the dry white pleasant if just a little acid, the 'medium red' soft but honest. Shipped by Martino of Verona, they seem to be minor representatives of the region's Soave and Valpolicella. There is also a pink which is just dry enough.

Santa Helena. A light and dry white wine from the Peloponnese.

Santa Laura. Soft but dependable red and white table wines from the Peloponnese which are among the cheaper bottles in their home country and which even after their journey to the U.K. still compare well with a lot of far less honest wines.

Santa Maria. Brand name for English-bottled Spanish wines sold by Fine Fare and others. The red 'full bodied table wine' is dark and unpleasant and discouraged me from trying the three varieties of white.

Santenay. A fairly large commune at the southern extreme of the Côte d'Or which makes firm, fruity red wines of no great character but as yet also rather cheaper than the Burgundies from farther north.

Santiago. Brand name for Rioja wines marketed by Mackinlay-McPherson (Edinburgh): red, sweet or dry white and pink, at a uniform price. Also Yago Sant'gria, the traditional mix of red wine and citrus fruit – someone should be ashamed for the name alone.

Sardinia. In the past Sardinia has mostly provided strong wines for blending with those of the mainland. The new Italian laws are already diminishing the demand for such wines, and the island's production, now dominated by modern co-operatives, is changing gear accordingly. Some of its better ordinaries have entered the export market under varietal names like Cannonau (a native white grape), Sangiovese (the reliable grape of Chianti) and especially Nuragus. The Malvasia dessert wines and the dry Vernaccia (a sort of natural sherry used equally as an aperitif or dessert wine) will probably find their way to us as well.

Sassella. ⟡ Valtellina.

Saumur. The hills around this Loire village have long produced dry, light but vigorous white wines with a fragrance and taste quite unlike any others of the Anjou region. They also produced Cabernet de Saumur, one of the few French pink wines I actually liked drinking. It was pale, bright and refreshing like a Weissherbst, but the AC was discontinued in 1974.

Saumur is now perhaps best known for the sparkling wines it produces in increasing quantities, 'better and cheaper than much indifferent and over-priced Champagne' said The Wine Society's centenary brochure. The good ones are indeed made by the méthode champenoise, but look hard at the label, for the success of the wine has prompted some producers to use the cheaper cuve close method.

Sauternes. A small area in the south of the Graves district, between Sauternes and Barsac, makes rich, sweet, golden and wholly marvellous white wines from Sémillon grapes affected by noble rot. Production is small and hazardous, and the cost correspondingly high. Unfortunately, the ordinary wines of the region are not even pale shadows of their grand cousins: they are sweet all right, but without the scent and the body.

Sauvignon. One of the finest species of white grapes, responsible for a great deal of white Bordeaux as well as for such individual wines as Pouilly-Fumé and Sancerre. It is also used most successfully in California for the best and fullest white wines there, and in Chile.

Savagnin. The name of several varieties of grapes. The Savagnin Blanc is also known as Traminer, the Savagnin Rosé is much better known as Gewürztraminer.

Savigny-lès-Beaune. A village at the top of the small river valley which separates Beaune from Aloxe. For the area it has an unusually low proportion of premier cru vineyards. This does not noticeably make its wines any worse than those of Beaune, but it does help to keep their prices within our range.

Savoy. ⋄ Apremont; Seyssel.

Schaumwein. (G) Sparkling wine. ⋄ Sekt.

Scheurebe. A successful cross between Sylvaner and Riesling vines, thriving on poor soil, cropping more richly and earlier than the Riesling. Its bouquet especially is wholly unlike that of Müller-Thurgau, a popular cross of the same vines, but with the Riesling as the 'mother'. The best sweet wines of the Unterhaardt are made from this grape.

Schillerwein. A pink speciality of Württemberg, made from white and black grapes pressed together. The name is also used in Alsace for similar wines.

Schlossböckelheim. A small village on the Nahe, upstream from Kreuznach, which has both the most famous vineyard of the whole region (the Kupfergrube) and the largest co-operative. Its wines are pale, fresh and fragrant. Incidentally, the name of the place really is one word, but several labels seem intent on obtaining extra mileage from the 'château' image of writing it Schloss Böckelheim.

Schluck. Meaning 'a mouthful'. Popular dry white wine made in the Wachau district of Austria, mostly from the Sylvaner grape.

Sciatino. Brand name of Nicolas for a dry rosé.

Seaview. A small winery in the hills south of Adelaide making soft red wines from Shiraz grapes which are among the few Australian wines cheap enough to really deserve a place in this guide.

sec. (F) Dry. If used of Champagne it means slightly sweet.

secco; seco. (I; S) Dry.

sediment. Solid particles which settle in the bottle. A dark sediment caused by tannin contained in the colourants is often found in older red wines. It affects the taste if allowed to mix freely with the wine: ▷ decanting. A white crystalline deposit found in younger wines and caused by tartrates is quite harmless.

Sekt. Sparkling white wine made in Germany. 'Deutscher Sekt' has to be made mostly from German grapes, otherwise Sekt is anonymous in origin, distinguished only by names of producing firms which buy grapes wherever it suits them.

Sémillon. A grape producing white wines which are 'straw to gold' in colour. Its Californian produce is often very good, but in Australia its very wide use results in wines which are indifferent enough to be sold under such incompatible names as Riesling and Chablis. With the Riesling grape Sémillon shares a predilection for noble rot and consequently the capability to make lusciously sweet wines. Sauternes is its masterpiece.

Seppelt. One of the largest wine-producing firms in Australia, famous at home for the 'champagne wines' of its Great Western vineyards north-west of Melbourne. Abroad it is better known for the Cabernet wines from Barossa Valley.

Sercial. Name of the grape from which the only light and almost-dry type of Madeira is made.

Serra. Not really a brand name, but that of the Lisbon shippers whose Justina range is better known in the U.K. The white Serra (in a hock bottle) and the red (in a Burgundy bottle) are both one-year-olds from the Torres Vedras region north of Lisbon.

servir frais. (F) Serve chilled.

Setúbal. ¢ Faisca; Portugal.

Seyssel. A sparkling wine made by the méthode champenoise a little way down the Rhône from Geneva. It is gaining popularity as a cheapish substitute for the real thing.

Seyve-Villard. Of the various hybrid vines developed by this experimental vintner the one which bears the number 5/276 has become very popular in regions with a distinct lack of sun, especially upstate New York and England. It grows well on chalk, has a high yield and an equally high acidity.

sharp. Said when the taste of a wine is dominated by its acidity.

sherry. The best and certainly the only famous wine of Spain, made in the extreme south-east, between Jerez de la Frontera and Sanlúcar de Barrameda, a small port at the mouth of the Guadalquivir. Its grape is the Palomino, which on the reflecting chalk ground of the area gets cooked from both sides by an uncomfortably hot sun. Crushed rather than pressed, and separated from its skins almost immediately, it is made into delicate white wines which (however good some of them may taste when very young) mostly go straight into the top layer of a solera system, to be aged and blended in mysterious and guarded ways until they emerge as the more or less individual brand on some six hundred different labels. Shipments from Jerez are no longer permitted in bulk but only in bottle: this has recently put up the price of most sherries.

Shiraz. The New World name for Syrah varieties – nothing to do with the Persian vineyards sung by Omar Kháyyám.

Sicily. The hot and fertile island at the southern point of the Italian boot, where 'what is not mountain is taken up by vineyards and orchards and olive groves', and where the Greeks made wine three thousand years ago. These days, its wines are slowly making their way back into the market, as new methods and ever-larger wineries improve the quality of what used to be sent north for blending. The sweet dessert wines, Malvasia and Marsala, have long been famous. Among the table wines, the rather heavy reds are usually better than the whites, but ⋄ Corvo.

Sidi Larbi. The best known of Moroccan red wines, and one of the very few sold in the U.K. under its proper regional name. It is made in the coastal hills west of the Middle Atlas, between Rabat and Casablanca.

sirvase frio. (S) Serve chilled.

Soave. A pale yellow wine made on the southern slopes of the hills between Vicenza and Verona, mostly from Garganega grapes which are separated from their skins. Firm and well-balanced, but of greatly varying quality, especially in the double-litre export market.

SODAP. ⋄ Cyprus.

soft. Describes smooth-tasting wine with low tannin content.

Sogrape. ⋄ Vinho Verde.

soil. Different types of soil can completely change the

character of wines produced from the same grape. Chalk and limestone are the great soils for white wines. Gravel and sand reflect heat to help develop the fruit in seasons or climates with little sun. Clay makes for full rich grapes but presents drainage problems. Good drainage is a crucial factor for any site, whatever the soil. Poor but loose soil will make the vines root deeper, making them less dependent on changes of weather.

solera. A system of butts of wine, arranged in groups according to age. The groups are known as criaderas, and usually there are at least six such groups in a system. Wine is bottled only from the criadera containing the oldest wine. This criadera is then replenished from the next oldest, and so on, until the last one is topped up with young wine. The amount of wine bottled at any one time is very small compared to the total content of even a single criadera, and the overall quality of the blends therefore remains remarkably constant. Madeira labels often give a date for their solera: this is the year the first wine was put in, and so indicates no more than how long that particular solera has been going.

Solitaire. Brand name of the Wine Growers' Association (London) for very cheap French ordinaries ingeniously described to make them sound like A C surplus wines: red 'akin to mellow Rhône', white 'hinting of Burgundy' and rosé 'with much affinity to Anjou'.

Sordo Lopez. Brand name for a range of very cheap but honest Spanish wine bottled by Phillips Newman and sold through chains like Unwins: three whites (the dry one being the best for most purposes), a red and a pink.

Soussans. The wines of this Haut-Médoc parish downstream from Margaux can and often do use the latter name. Those that only use the village name are not necessarily any worse, just more modest.

South Africa. Cape Province, at least, produces some decent table wines at Stellenbosch, Paarl and Tulbagh – but only vast quantities of indifferent, cheap sherry-style wines seem to reach the U.K. About half the country's grape harvest is distilled into the brandies which are the national drink.

Spain. The last country left in Europe with a complete lack of control over the methods and quality of its wine production – except for sherry, which is very rigorously controlled by the growers rather than the state, and Catalonia, which applies different standards to almost anything anyway. This said, it should also be acknowledged that a great deal of very drinkable wine comes from Spain, especially the Rioja, much of it made by producers who buy grapes rather than grow them. Unfortunately for us, what is sold in the U.K. under brand names like Corrida (what else?) or by food chains like Sainsbury's is no recommendation at all.

Spanna. Local name for the Nebbiolo grape and its wines, used around the Lago Maggiore in northern Piedmont.

sparkling wine. Wine drawn from the vat before fermentation is complete and then, with the addition of sugar and a yeast culture, subjected to a second fermentation in a tightly closed space – be this a bottle (méthode champenoise) or a tank (cuve close). A very few wines are made sparkling during the first fermentation, notably Asti Spumante.

Spätburgunder. A small, violet grape with strong aroma, the German version of the Pinot Noir. It is used on the Ahr and in Baden-Württemberg for the finest German reds, light in colour but full and fruity.

Spätlese. (G) Wine made from late-gathered grapes. Under German wine laws its must-weight has to be about 80 Oechsle, which puts it one up on the Kabinett classification.

Springton. ▷ Barossa Valley.

spritzig. (G) 'Lively' because of a very little carbon dioxide.

spumante. (I) Sparkling.

Staufenberg, Schloss. ▷ Baden.

Steinwein. Long the common name for all the better white wines from the Würzburg (Franken) area, but now by law confined to those of the Stein vineyard which is probably the biggest in all Germany.

still. Not sparkling.

storing. If wine is to be stored for any length of time, it is best to find a place for it which comes as near as possible to these conditions: an even temperature, preferably between 45 and 55°F; no direct daylight, let alone sun; and room to stack the bottles lying down flat, never with the top raised (if the cork is not kept moist it will shrink and allow air to spoil the wine).

sulphur. In the form of sulphur dioxide, sulphur is sometimes used in sweet wines to prevent further fermentation in the bottle. It produces an unpleasant smell when the bottle is opened and can affect the taste as well.

Sungurlu. Name of a native Turkish white grape and of the wines it makes, dry but with a strong taste (not unlike resin although certainly not of it) which I found very easy to acquire.

supermarkets. The words 'supermarket plonk' have gained derogatory currency, and on the whole with ample justification. Some shops seem determined to keep the reputation of cheap wines, especially Spanish ones, unnecessarily low. The Co-ops, Fine Fare and Sainsbury's dole out the most awful blends, in various colours, and all at prices for which with a bit of trouble you could find much better wines that you would actually enjoy. Sainsbury's really cheap Moroccan Red, on the other hand, is excellent. Dingle's and Safeway's cheap brands are merely indifferent, not really bad. Dingle's is actually called Plonk. Ambitious ranges of French wines are to be found at Tesco Stores (⇨ De Georges) and at Waitrose. Fine Fare market the Fleuron range of controlled Bordeaux wines and the most interesting selection of medium-priced wines is offered by Marks & Spencer. Comments from users of supermarket and similar brand wines will be most welcome.

Switzerland. The Swiss vineyards are largely extensions of those in neighbouring regions: in the north of Baden and Württemberg, along the Jura (canton Neuchâtel) and around Lake Geneva (canton Vaud) of the French mountain vineyards, and in the Italian-speaking Ticino of the northern Italian lake district. The only 'independent' region is that of the upper Rhône valley (canton Valais). Until recently the country produced mostly white wines. Neuchâtel specializes in slightly sparkling ones, Vaud and Valais produce excellent table wines like Fendant. Under economic pressure more and more black grapes are introduced and the results are promising. The Dôle mountain region near Geneva uses Gamay grapes to effect, and the Ticino sells its red wines under the varietal name of its main grape, the Merlot. The latter are soft but just about pleasant; all are drunk young.

Sykes scale. The Customs & Excise instrument for determining the percentage of alcohol in a liquor. Its readings are based on the English proof system (⇨ proof) and go from 0 for distilled water to about 175 for absolute alcohol.

Sylvaner. A high-yielding white grape, medium-sized, closely packed, green in colour, which is not very demanding as regards soil. It is the main grape in German wine production outside the Moselle and Rhine regions, and is also widely used in Alsace, Austria and eastern Europe. Its wines seldom reach the quality of good Riesling, the better wines of Franken being the exception.

Syrah. The great black grape of the Rhône, responsible for the dark wines of Hermitage and the Côte Rôtie. As Shiraz, one of its versions is used for equally dark high-tannin wines in California, and under that same name or as Hermitage it is the common grape of Australia alongside (and often mixed with) Cabernet Sauvignon.

szamorodni. (H) 'Ordinary' in the sense that no special selection was involved as with aszu.

Szekszárd. A village in south-western Hungary surrounded by low hills which produce the driest of the country's red wines, Szekszárdi Vörös (literally 'red from Szekszárd'), sometimes known as Szekszárdi Bikavér to recall its mellower rival from Eger at the opposite end of the country.

Szürkebarat. ⟡ Badacsony.

T

table wine. Ordinary wine for everyday use. Under English Customs & Excise regulations it is any wine 'not exceeding 25 per cent proof spirit', which means a maximum alcohol content of 14 volume per cent.

Tafelwein. (G) Corresponds to 'vin ordinaire', everyday wine which need meet only minimum requirements. No vineyard name can be used for it.

Tahbilk, Château. One of the few remaining quality vineyards in Victoria. About seventy-five miles due north of Melbourne, near a place called Tabilk (the h is as spurious as the château), they make very good red wines from the usual Cabernet and Shiraz mixtures, and better whites from the very unusual Marsanne. All are among the cheaper Australian wines available in the U.K.

Taluna. Brand name for a remarkably indifferent range of Spanish wines marketed in the U.K. by Capital Wine & Travers (London). Red, pink and three sweetnesses of white come at a uniform price in bottles, litres, double-litres and five-gallon containers. You save, but very little, at each step.

tannin. An organic material deriving from the gallic acid and found in the skin and stones of the grape. It is an important factor in preserving red wines (white wines have little or none) but too much of it makes for an astringent taste.

tartaric acid. One of the natural acids in wine, and the one which gives what is usually called a 'rough' taste.

tartrates

tartrates. Clear crystals formed by the separation of super-
fluous tartaric acid mainly into potassium bitartrate, often
after exposure to lowish temperatures. They do not result
in loss of quality: the drop in acidity may even improve the
wine.

tasting. To develop any knowledge not just of wine but,
more important, of your own likes and dislikes, it is necessary to try as many wines as you can, and to judge them by
colour, by smell and by taste: eye, nose and mouth. There
is no need to make a ritual of these proceedings, but it is a
serious business all the same for in terms of wine you will
have to become your own investment broker. There is an
excellent (if very serious) chapter on the techniques of
tasting in *The Penguin Book of Wines*, and Michael Broad-
bent has written a whole book on the subject which is
sold by his own firm, Christie's (Wine Department) in
London.

tasting clubs. These can provide a relatively cheap way to
greater experience and knowledge. One bottle provides
roughly twenty to twenty-four 'tastes', therefore the ideal
number of club members would be about that. This means
that for 50p each you can taste half a dozen reasonably
priced wines, and for an annual subscription of a fiver
you could organize really interesting quarterly meetings.
Any good wine merchant would be glad to advise on
choice.

Tavel. The best known rosé until the advent of Mateus. It
is made in Gard, on the right bank of the Rhône just south
of Lirac (which makes a similar wine) and opposite
Châteauneuf du Pape. Its colour, the lack of body politely
called 'elegance', and the 'fruity' flavour which is reminis-
cent of no particular fruit (let alone grape) have long
summed up everything I happen to dislike about French
pink wines in general.

tawny. Descriptive term for port aged in the wood for a long time, usually ten to fifteen years, during which time it fades to brick red and develops a light and delicate taste.

Tebourba. ⟡ Tunisia.

Tekel. ⟡ Turkey.

Terlano. A very good dry wine of pale greenish-yellow colour made in the Alto Adige around the village which gave its name to both the wine and the main grape.

Tesco Stores. ⟡ De Georges; Franchette.

Tessala. A hill region south of Oran which produces some of the best Algerian wine, full and smooth reds with a slight raspberry flavour and a good colour.

tête de cuvée. (F) First drawing-off from the vat: the best-quality wine.

Ticino. ⟡ Switzerland.

tinto. (S and P) Red.

tiré sur lie. (F) Wine which is not racked off the lees before it is bottled. Treated this way the wine retains a stronger fruit flavour and usually a small measure of carbon dioxide (which may be increased by malolactic fermentation in the bottle). The wines of Neuchâtel are made this way, and Muscadet 'sur lie' is quite superior to the ordinary one.

Tirol. Only a little wine now comes from the Austrian Tirol, south of Innsbruck. Most of it is white, light, undistinguished but pleasant enough. What used to be Tirol south of the Brenner Pass is now Italian: ⟡ Alto Adige.

Tocai. ⟡ Friuli.

Tokay. One of the world's most famous dessert wines – but that is only one end of a large range of Tokay wines, made from the Furmint grape in the far north-eastern corner of Hungary. Tokaji Furmint is almost a table wine, slightly sweet but spicy. Tokaji Szamorodni (meaning 'as it comes') is made from a later gathering of grapes: the dry version is excellent, also as an aperitif. Tokaji Aszu is the famous one. It is made by adding a strong special pressing from grapes affected by noble rot to the ordinary must, in varying quantities, to produce increasingly sweet wines at prices which move correspondingly further outside the range of everyday drinking.

Tokay d'Alsace. ⇨ Pinot Gris.

Toro, El. Brand name of Wine Agencies London for Spanish red and (dry) white wines which come in bottles and 'large bottles' of unspecified content but reasonable quality.

Touraine. The wine-producing area around Tours which includes the valleys of the Loire, the Cher and the Indre. Just above its main town are the white wine regions of Vouvray and Montlouis, best known for their slightly sparkling 'vins vifs'. Farther down the river lie the only good red wine villages of the entire Loire, Bourgeuil and Chinon.

Tour (du Pin) Figeac, Château la. ⇨ Saint-Émilion.

Trakya. Name of a light red wine, and of a white made from Sémillon grapes, produced in Trakya (Thrace), the European province of Turkey (from which Dionysus is supposed to have brought the culture of the vine to the unsuspecting world).

Traminer. Variety of the Savagnin Blanc grape much used in the Mittelhaardt region of the Palatinate, in Baden and in the regions on either side of the Hungarian–Yugoslav border. In Alsace the name was also used for lesser Gewürztraminer wines until this use was outlawed at the end of 1972. ⇨ Alto Adige.

Trebbiano. One of Italy's best white grapes. Taking its name from the Trebbia river (which runs into the Po near Piacenza) it is probably a native of that region but is grown throughout all Emilia-Romagna. Its one really great wine is Orvieto, from farther south; others go by the varietal name, often without any indication of place. In the Lazio region it makes good wines in conjunction with Malvasia grapes. In France it is known as Ugni Blanc.

Trier. Not in itself a wine-producing town, but very much the centre of large holdings (especially in Saar estates) and therefore often found on labels. The cathedral (Hohe Domkirche, prefixing all its wines with Dom), the Friedrich Wilhelm Gymnasium (where Karl Marx went to school) and various religious bodies are important and reliable producers.

Trittenheim. A long steep land-tongue in a bend of the Moselle, not too far from Trier, is the beginning of the Middle Moselle region where all the best Moselle wines are grown. Its best-known vineyards, Altärchen on both banks and Apotheke on the east bank across from the village, are both conglomerates of smaller estates marketing their wine under the name of the best-known.

trocken. (G) Dry. Under German wine law, such dry wines may not have more than four grammes of unfermented sugar per litre.

Trollinger. A big late-ripening black grape which flourishes on heavy chalk in the warmer parts of Germany, especially Württemberg. Its wines should be drunk young.

Troplong-Mondot, Château. ◊ Saint-Émilion.

Tsinandali. ◊ Georgia.

Tsingtao. ◊ China.

Tuella. Brand name for three colours of good table wine from the Douro valley in northern Portugal. Marketed in the U.K. by Harvey's of Bristol.

Tunisia. The Tunisian vineyards occupy a very small area around the capital and on the Maouin peninsula towards Ras el Tib (Cap Bon). Production is controlled very strictly and maintains the high standards of French regulations. The Teboura region ('Coteaux de Carthage') produces red wines of AC quality, and of the 16,000 hectare on the peninsula about 3,000 around Grombalia and coastal Kelibia also reach A C standards.

Turkey. The vineyard acreage here is enormous, but few grapes are made into wine: 60 per cent is simply eaten, fresh or as sultanas, and another 37 per cent is used for juice. The wine-producing areas are scattered all through the country, from the European province of Trakya, along the Aegean coast (especially around Izmir, the former Smyrna), to the Anatolian highlands. Tekel, the State Monopolies, run seventeen large wineries which are responsible for most of what is exported: the red Buzbağ and Kalebağ, the white Narbağ, Sungurlu and Ürgüp. An interesting range of white wines is handled by the Doluca concern, more ordinary wines by Aral.

Tuscany. The province either of Florence, Siena, Pisa and the Italian Renaissance – or of Chianti. The region (which officially includes the island of Elba) produces mostly red wines made from Sangiovese or Brunello grapes, nearly always mixed with one or two other varieties in varying proportions. The whites, by and large, are of little consequence except for the few which used to be called 'white Chianti' until this name was outlawed.

U

Ugni Blanc. One of the dominant white grapes of southern France, second only to the Clairette. Under the curious name St-Émilion it is also responsible for most Cognac, and under the even more curious name 'white Hermitage' it makes the better white wines of Australia. ◊ Trebbiano.

ullage. The amount of wine by which a bottle may be short of its original content if a faulty cork has allowed evaporation. This usually results in loss of quality as well. It is an important word to look for in bin end and auction lists.

Unterhaardt. This northernmost sub-district of the Rheinpfalz produces the sweeter wines of the region, the best of which are made from the Scheurebe.

Untertürkheim. ◊ Württemberg.

Ürgüp. A white wine from Cappadocia which derives its name from a village near Turkey's main river, the Kizil Irmak. It is made from the native Emir grape.

Ürzig. On the left bank of the Moselle, where the usual slate ground is mixed with clay and the resulting wines have a strong flavour. This is reflected in the name of the most famous vineyard here, the Würzgarten (spice garden). The best known of Ürzig's cheaper wines is Schwarzlay, which I find rather thin.

U.S.A. Only two wine-producing areas in the States are worthy of note: upstate New York and California. The Finger Lakes of New York moderate the state's land climate somewhat, but the vine has a hard time all the same and it has long been assumed that only the native American varieties like Concord and Catawba would be sufficiently hardy. Recently such hybrids as the Seyve-Villard 5/276 have shown that this is not so, but the wines produced in the region remain rather acid and nowhere near the standards obtained in California (for which see its separate entry).

U.S.S.R. In the 1950s and early 1960s Russia more than doubled the area of its vineyards. Most of the wine they produce is for home consumption, and the native taste is for sweet wines. The Crimea and Georgia produce very good dry table wines, and Moldavia continues to make the same wines it made when it was part of Romania: dry white Fetjaska (Fetească) and fruity red Negru de Purkar. ⇨ also Armenia, Azerbaijan and Georgia.

V

Vacqueyras. ⇨ Côtes du Rhône-Villages.

Valais. ⇨ Switzerland.

Val d'Aosta. The largely French-speaking region north of Turin and just south of the Alps, from which Francis I already imported wine. It boasts the highest vineyards in Europe, at Morgex. Their white wine and the Nebbiolo red of Carema are among the few ever found with specific place-names attached.

Valdepeñas. Centre of the extensive wine-producing area in the plain of La Mancha, south of Madrid. Its red wines, light in both colour and body but strong in alcohol, and the much fuller golden whites were for a long time the carafe wines of Spain. They are now becoming those of the U.K. as well.

Valpantena. The slightly lesser and lighter brother of Valpolicella.

Valpolicella. The best, and best-known, red wine from the east side of Lake Garda: beautiful to look at, full in flavour, just a little sharp (not so noticeable when drunk cool on a summer day). One of the most reliable wines in the two-litre market, it is made from the same grapes as Bardolino and Valpantena.

Valtellina. The valley of the Adda river, east of Lake Como, produces some very good red wines from the black Nebbiolo grape. The more ordinary ones are sold under the simple name of the region, the better ones (in ascending order of quality) as Fracia, Grumello and Sassella. Inferno is made from a mixture of grapes and has a different fruity taste. The Valtellina wines are known as Veltliners in Switzerland, but have no connection with the grape of that name, of course.

varietal names. Names which derive from the principal grape variety used in making the wine they are applied to. In Europe, the one most frequently used is Riesling. In the United States, and in many countries exporting large quantities of ordinary wines, varietal names are used more than those denoting exact origin. In the U.K. market, too, varietal names are becoming more common: ▷ brand names.

Vaud. ▷ Switzerland.

VDQS. ▷ vin délimité de qualité supérieure.

Veltliner. More precisely Grüner Veltliner. The best native white grape of Austria, especially the Burgenland district where its wines are drunk almost before they are finished. It has a distinctive high fruit flavour. It is also used, in several varieties with as many different names, in most of eastern Europe and the Balkan countries.

vendange. (F) The grape harvest.

vendange tardive. (F) Alsatian term for wine made from grapes which are gathered late, as in the German Spätlese.

vendemmia; vendimia. (I; S) Vintage.

Veneto. The better wines of the Veneto (the province which used to be Venice's inland possession) all come from the volcanic hills of Lake Garda, north of Verona. They are among the best wines of Italy, whether white (Soave) or red (Bardolino and Valpolicella).

Verdelho. Name of the grape from which one of the less sweet types of Madeira is made.

Verdicchio dei Castelli di Jesi. Perhaps the best of all Italian dry white wines, full-flavoured and rather high in alcohol content. Made in the Esino valley, north of Ancona, mostly from Verdicchio grapes, it comes in a characteristic fancy bottle with a narrow waist.

Verdignan, Château. ◊ Saint-Seurin-de-Cadourne.

Vermouth. Generic name for fortified white wine given flavour or colour with herbs and aromatics. The practice is an old one, and has always had wormwood as its main ingredient. The present commercial vermouths originate in the French and Italian Alps, with Turin and Marseilles as the capital producers. Italian vermouths tend to be the sweeter ones, with about 15 per cent alcohol and even more sugar. By comparison, French vermouth is dry: it usually has only a quarter as much sugar, goes easier on ingredients like cinnamon but heavier on wormwood. A great number of Alpine herbs can be used to produce different tastes, the most distinctive of which is that of Chambéry vermouth. The oldest proprietary name seems to be Carpano, which has recently entered its third century.

Vernaccia. Name of an Italian grape which produces light and rather delicate white wines in various parts of the country, and a very good stronger one in the Tuscan hills of San Gimignano. All are known by the grape name followed by an indication of origin. ◊ also Sardinia.

Veronello. Brand name for three colours of very drinkable northern Italian wines claiming to be no more than 'vino da pasto'. The pink is harder to get simply because it is sold in the kind of shop where the distinction between rosso and rosato is too much for the staff (notably in London Co-ops).

Veuve Aubie. Brand name of Wine Agencies London for a sparkling Saumur which is reasonable in price because it is made by the cheap cuve close method.

Veuve du Vernay. A widely sold brand of cheapish sparkling wine, white or pink, which officially come brut or demi-sec: neither is dry at all.

Victoria Wine. ⋄ Castella; wine-store chains.

Vieux Ceps. Brand name of Nicolas for the heavier of their red blends.

Villa Antinori. Traditionally, this is the best red wine of the Antinori house: a Chianti classico. It is now used for a 'dry Tuscan white, remarkably fruity for an Italian wine': a 'white Chianti' that got away.

Villandry. This small village on the Loire below Tours has long been famous for the lovingly reconstructed Renaissance gardens of its château. It will gain no new fame from the nasty cheap white wine sold under its name.

viña. (S) Vineyard.

Vinado. ⋄ Barrera.

Vin de Corse. ⋄ Corsica.

Vin de France. Brand name for the better range of French wines of the Wine Growers' Association (London). The three whites and three reds all seem to be blended from good regional wines of AC rather than VDQS standards.

vin délimité de qualité supérieure. The second rank of controlled French wines. The appellation is mainly applied to good wines which used to be of local or regional interest only. It is precisely these wines which are providing an ever larger percentage of our everyday consumption. This does not mean, however, that they also form a limitless part of French production: not more than perhaps 5 or 6 per cent can claim VDQS status. The winegrowers' associations make recommendations for wines to be accepted to the appellation, but the National Institute controlling the whole 'appellations contrôlées' system has to grant the status.

vin de marque. (F) Wine which is sold under a proprietary (brand) name only. Usually blended.

vin de masă. (R) Table wine.

vin de pays. (F) At present, this is still a popular name for ordinary wines (Landwein in German) of no particular character or status, but from 1980 on it will be the name of a third and lowest controlled class of French wines. The southern provinces of Aude, Garde and Hérault, responsible for half the country's total wine production but largely without ACs, have already been allotted the larger number of these new controlled names: 13, 11 and 18 respectively, out of a total of 67.

vin des sables. (F) Wine made in the few remaining, usually coastal vineyards where an attempt was made to combat phylloxera by rooting the vines in deep sand in which, it was thought, the bug did not like to live. Aigues-Mortes still produces some which I have come to like.

vin doux naturel. ◊ Roussillon.

vin du Midi. (F) A common name for ordinary wines from Languedoc and Roussillon.

viñedo. (S) Vineyard.

vin fou. (F) Sparkling wine, especially the cheap but pleasant one from Arbois in the Jura which is quite simply bottled before the end of its original fermentation.

Vin Gough. Brand name of Gough Brothers (London) for a London-bottled range of French wines which go under simple regional AC names, and for two Rieslings from Hungary and Yugoslavia.

vin gris. (F) The Jura version of Weissherbst. The one most widely available in the U.K., Cendré de Novembre (shipped, as is most Jura wine, by Henri Maire), is a good example: very pale, rather sharp, but a fine wine for summer drinking. Morocco makes some very similar wines usually just labelled Gris.

vinha. (P) Vineyard.

vinho de mesa. (P) Table wine.

Vinho Verde. 'Green' wine (made of underripe grapes) which is rich in malic acid. The reds are very bright, the whites almost colourless. They are what the Germans call spritzig: they give the sensation of a sparkle without actually being sparkling wines. The Entre-Minho-e-Douro region in northern Portugal produces a great variety of these wines, and the official name of this região demarcada is now simply Vinho Verde. The most widely distributed ones in the U.K. are Gatão (Grants of St James's) and Casal Garcia (Sogrape, who did such a stunning job making their Mateus Rosé a household word). My own favourite is Aveleda, which unlike the other two is always a white – not that this makes much difference since nobody seems to bother importing the red ones anyway.

vin jaune. ◊ flor.

Vin Lore. Brand name for a range of rather indifferent Yugoslav wines marketed in the U.K. by Teltscher Brothers (London). All four are rather sweet.

vino da pasto. (I) Table wine.

Vino de Catalonia. This brand name of Sainsbury's seems to have replaced their 'Spanish' series without doing much for the quality of the product.

vino de cosecha propia. (S) Wine made by the vineyard's owner.

vino de mesa, vino de pasto. (S). Table wine.

vin ordinaire. (F) Wine for everyday use, not governed by the AC laws.

vino santo (I) Dessert wine made from grapes dried in the sun after they were harvested.

vintage. The wine of one particular year. On American labels, a date only indicates the year of bottling unless the word vintage specifically precedes it.

More generally, the word can also mean the grape harvest itself.

vintage character. ⟳ crusted.

vintage charts. Very rough guides to the quality of wines from different regions in different years, distinguishing between 'good' and 'bad' years. There are so many individual exceptions that about the only thing one can be sure of is a high price for generally recognized top years. For the cheaper wines, especially those on restaurant lists, it is perhaps better to remember the bad vintages than the good ones: 1963, 1965 and especially 1968 were bad years both in France and in Germany; 1972 is good but had a small crop and fetches absurd prices, and 1974 seems to have been a bad year for all French wines, especially Beaujolais.

vintage port. The unblended wine of a particularly good year, bottled early. Different producers may make vintage port in different years, according to their own wisdom. The last generally declared vintage was 1970.

vin vif. (F) Slightly sparkling wine.

Vista, La. Brand name of Gilbey Vintners for an unusually wide range of honest Spanish wines. The two Riojas (dry white and 'medium full red') are light but good. The 'Catalonia medium dry white' poses a problem: it proclaims itself 'denominación de origen Tarragona' but this has long been a name which could only be applied to fortified sweet wines (the La Vista one is dry and delicate). The pink wine comes from Valencia, and the range is completed by a sweet white and a 'full red' from an unspecified region (probably Aragon).

Vitis labrusca. ⟳ foxy; phylloxera.

Vitis vinifera. The one species of vine out of about forty from which good wine can be made. There are some five thousand varieties, and new ones are still being created by cross-breeding.

Vollrads, Schloss. ⟳ Winkel.

Volnay. The vineyards of Volnay continue those of Pommard on one side, of Meursault on the other. Their white wine goes under the name of Meursault, and Meursault's reds use the name Volnay. There are those (and I am one) who insist that the red wines of Volnay are preferable to those of Pommard, even if they are similar in colour, smell, and life-span (which is seldom more than eight to ten years).

vörös. (H) Red.

Vouvray. The chalky hills of the small river Brenne (which runs into the Loire at Vouvray) are best known nowadays for producing endless quantities of well-made and drinkable sparkling wine. What is forgotten is that these sparkling wines are made from the failures of the region: wines with too high a level of acidity. The best still wines of the region are sweet and firm and have the unusual ability to improve in the bottle for several decades.

W

Wachau. Area along the Danube, near Krems in Austria, which produces a variety of good white wines. The driest is Schluck, made from Sylvaner grapes. Wines made from an Austrian grape called Grüner Veltliner are high-flavoured, golden and full-bodied. The Dürnstein co-operative, to which over a thousand growers in this region belong, is the largest producer.

Wachenheim. On the Deutsche Weinstrasse, a few miles south of Bad Dürkheim. A rather large number of individual vineyards produces white wines of quality and delicate flavour, nowhere near as rich as those of neighbouring Forst.

Wachstum. (G) Estate, vineyard.

Waitrose. The food branch of the John Lewis partnership now runs forty-eight licensed supermarkets (none north of Birmingham) and sells a large range of wines under its own name. Some of these are self-explanatory ACs, but the ordinaires (in litre and two-litre bottles) are not. The Vin de Table, in three colours, is French. The Vin Rouge is French as well, but the Vin Blanc and Vin Rosé have long been Hungarian, and the Carafe Rouge is a double-litre wine from Algeria. The labels do not specify the volume content of the bottles.

Wehlen. On the left bank of the Moselle, but with vineyards across the river continuing those of Bernkastel and Graach and producing wines of the same high quality. Sonnenuhr is its best-known large estate.

Weingarten, Weingut. (G) Estate.

Weinkellerei. (G) Wine cellar.

Weissherbst. (G) Pink wine made from black grapes (Portugieser or Spätburgunder) in the manner of a white wine, that is from the pressed-out juice only. Usually pale, almost smoky, very fresh. To be drunk young, and cold. German wine lists include Weissherbsts among the red wines.

Weisswein. (G) White wine.

white wine. Wine made from the juice pressed out of (usually) green or yellow-skinned grapes. The must often has a high sugar content, and not all of this may be converted into alcohol since the fermenting yeasts die when the alcohol concentration becomes too high. The residual sugar gives the richer white wines their characteristic sweetness and grape flavour.

wine. 'The alcoholic beverage obtained from the juice of freshly gathered grapes, the fermentation of which has been carried through in the district of its origin and according to local tradition and practice', says the Wine & Spirit Association of Great Britain. One rather glaring flaw in this definition is taken care of by the French legal definition, which insists on 'fresh grapes or the juice of fresh grapes'.

Wine Agencies (London). ◊ Sans Chichi; Toro; Veuve Aubie.

Wine Growers' Association. ◊ Solitaire; Vin de France.

wine laws. The legal guarantees for the origin and quality of wine have in recent years been revised to much stricter standards than before, and they are rigidly enforced in all the main producing countries.

The basics of the whole system derive from the French classification which was first formally set down for the International Exhibition of Industrial Products, Paris 1855, sponsored by Napoleon III. This famous list of crus classés, based on the prices their wine had fetched over the preceding century, has undergone few changes but has seen a considerable expansion in the 'appellation contrôlée' system, which is under constant supervision and revision.

Germany, too, has an easy and reliable system of classification partly based on long traditions but considerably tightened by the laws of 1971 – see the two entries under Qualitätswein.

The Italian system of 'denominazione' was announced in 1963 but is only slowly coming into effect. As there was no strong traditional framework to build on, it was left to the growers' organizations in each district to sort out their problems and submit the solutions for approval to a central body. Where these associations already had tight controls (the Chianti region, for instance) the new system came into operation very quickly, but most of southern Italy just has not bothered yet.

wine merchants. A good wine merchant is the quickest route to getting what you will like at a price you can afford. They are hard to find, but easy to spot, because for a start they will not be snotty to earnest if ignorant beginners.

Wine Society. For the serious beginner this is one of the better places to start, although the membership fee is no longer negligible. The half-yearly lists still include a large number of cheaper wines, all carefully and reliably described.

At the really cheap end are The Society's Carafe Wines: except perhaps for the dry white these are the kind of wines I cannot drink for long, or on their own. The Society's Vin Rouge (no. 1 for 'claret-style', no. 2 for 'Burgundy-style') is good value, The Society's Claret even more so, even if its price has risen sharply. The Society's Burgundy reflects the general price tendency for the genre, but is a true Pinot Noir and very drinkable indeed.

wine-store chains. The last decade or so has seen radical changes in the British attitude towards wine drinking, and the barometer of these changes is the emergence of extensive networks of outlets. There are still only a very few chains that can claim to be 'national', and most of these are backed by big brewers and distillers: the 630 shops of Peter Dominic and Westminster Wine by International, the huge Victoria Wine (with or without Tylers) plus the more recent Wine Market and Wineways stores (a total of 986) by Allied, who also own the leading firm of shippers, Grants of St James's. The empire of Augustus Barnett is steadily spreading wider, but a substantial percentage of its one hundred shops is still in London. The Midlands can boast several medium-sized chains of their own: T. F. Ashe & Nephew extend ever farther from their Merseyside base, Arthur Cooper have entered the area from a Bristol stronghold; Merseyside has Mackies; Birmingham is saturated with Good Cheer Cellars, Wine Sellers and the stores of Morris, Whittals and the Co-op. Both Galleon Wine (with its parent Wine Sellers the second largest chain in the country, with 955 shops) and Goldfinch Wine Stores cover the country farther north. The trouble with most chain stores (or supermarket drinks counters) is not so much their selection of wines as the ignorance of their staff: a specialized shop should offer knowledgeable advice as part of its service.

Winkel. Almost unknown but for the Schloss Vollrads estate, a very large private vineyard which omits the place name from its labels.

Winzergenossenschaft, Winzerverein. (G) A wineproducers' co-operative.

Württemberg. This old duchy includes most of the Neckar valley, with Stuttgart as its most important town. It produces mostly rather thin red wines, from a variety of grapes growing on chalk and red marl soils. Cannstatt ('Zückerle') and Untertürkheim (both suburbs of Stuttgart) and Lauffen are the names most often met with. Pink specialities of the region are Weissherbst and Schillerwein.

Würzburg. Centre of the wine-producing villages of Franken, with some of the most famous vineyards within its own city limits (Stein and Leisten) and also the offices of the greatest producers (Bürgerspital and Juliusspital).

X

Xynisteri. The native white grape of Cyprus, and hence
the name of a very nice dry wine from the Paphos end of
the island's wine region.

Y

Yugoslavia. Produces enormous quantities of wine, ranking about tenth in world production, and at the moment provides perhaps the best value for money in the cheaper wine range, especially in whites but also in some unusual reds.

In the north, below Austria, the provinces of Slovenia and Croatia use Italian (Olasz) Riesling, Muscat, Malvasia and Pinot Bijeli (Pinot Blanc) to make light wines with the fruity taste of their northern neighbours. These wines usually go under the grape name, prefixed with that of one of the large producing combines like Malena, or of a place like Ljutomer or Maribor.

The whole of the Dalmatian coast (and its islands) produces wines from small vineyards, with great local differences: strong reds like Dingač, very individual whites like Grk, and sweet wines like Prošek.

In the south-east, Serbia and Macedonia, the wines are more predominantly red. The standard grape here is Prokupac: its very dark wines are often blended with those of the softer Plovdina. The big co-operatives throughout the country increasingly use newly imported French vines.

Z

Zell. On the right bank of the river, downstream from the Middle Moselle region, Zell has just about the last important Moselle vineyards. Their wine is generally marketed as Schwarze Katz, once the name of the most illustrious Einzellage among them.

Zeltingen. On the Moselle, downstream from Graach. The biggest commune of the Middle Moselle, producing large quantities of very good wines which all the same never seem to attain quite the stunning quality of their upstream neighbours.

Žilavka. Dry but surprisingly full wine with a slightly smoky taste, made in the Neretva valley near Mostar, an old Turkish town in Bosnia. Of high alcohol content, it is made from the native grapes which give it their name.

Zinfandel. The mystery grape of California, where it is usually considered to be native despite the fact that it belongs to *Vitis vinifera* rather than the usual American varieties. It makes dry red table wines of moderate ageing ability, with a slight raspberry taste and a spicy aroma. Most of these are used for blending, but a few wineries market them under the varietal name.

Zwicker. Alsatian description for a blended wine. ⟡ Edelzwicker.

MORE ABOUT PENGUINS
AND PELICANS

Penguinews, which appears every month, contains details of all the new books issued by Penguins as they are published. From time to time it is supplemented by *Penguins in Print*, which is our complete list of almost 5,000 titles.

A specimen copy of *Penguinews* will be sent to you free on request. Please write to Dept EP, Penguin Books Ltd, Harmondsworth, Middlesex, for your copy.

In the U.S.A.: For a complete list of books available from Penguins in the United States write to Dept CS, Penguin Books, 625 Madison Avenue, New York, New York 10022.

In Canada: For a complete list of books available from Penguins in Canada write to Penguin Books Canada Ltd, 41 Steelcase Road West, Markham, Ontario.